INSIDE INCEST

Psychotherapy and Energy Healing Transform this therapist, and a guide for survivors

MADELINE A. GARNER

BALBOA.
PRESS

A DIVISION OF HAY HOUSE

Balboa Press books may be ordered through booksellers or by contacting:

Balboa Press
A Division of Hay House
1663 Liberty Drive
Bloomington, IN 47403
www.balboapress.com
1 (877) 407-4847

Because of the dynamic nature of the Internet, any web addresses or links contained in this book may have changed since publication and may no longer be valid. The views expressed in this work are solely those of the author and do not necessarily reflect the views of the publisher, and the publisher hereby disclaims any responsibility for them.

The author of this book does not dispense medical advice or prescribe the use of any technique as a form of treatment for physical, emotional, or medical problems without the advice of a physician, either directly or indirectly. The intent of the author is only to offer information of a general nature to help you in your quest for emotional and spiritual well-being. In the event you use any of the information in this book for yourself, which is your constitutional right, the author and the publisher assume no responsibility for your actions.

Any people depicted in stock imagery provided by Getty Images are models, and such images are being used for illustrative purposes only. Certain stock imagery © Getty Images.

Print information available on the last page.

ISBN: 978-1-9822-3108-8 (sc)
ISBN: 978-1-9822-3109-5 (hc)
ISBN: 978-1-9822-3110-1 (e)

Library of Congress Control Number: 2019909575

Balboa Press rev. date: 07/23/2019

CONTENTS

CONTENTS

TO THE SURVIVOR

If you are reading this book as an adult survivor of childhood sexual abuse, you may be experiencing a variety of uncomfortable feelings. Many survivors find counseling or therapy helpful for this. An experienced therapist can listen and help you understand and manage your emotions. Don't worry; they have heard it all. If you have no insurance or funds for counseling, you may be able to find a community mental health center near you.

If you feel you want to hurt yourself or end your life, please go to a hospital. If you are in an abusive adult relationship, there is help for that, too. Please avoid excessive use of alcohol and drugs or other risky behaviors.

If you already work on your healing, congratulations. If you read this book to understand a loved one's life as a survivor, or just to understand, welcome. All survivors are welcome.

Please give yourself love and consideration as you read. Take reading breaks. Share this book with your therapist if you have one. Find support from a partner, friend, or relative who is kind and sensitive to your feelings.

If you are an adult who was sexually abused as a child, remember that abuse is over. In spite of what happened to you in the past, you are a valuable person, and you belong here on this earth. You can learn to manage this new awareness of your past trauma, and you can feel much better than you do now. It will take some time to sort it out.

A special note to non-females: This book is aimed mostly at women because, according to research, the majority of incest which takes place in the home, involves little girls. However, any sexual abuse of others is just as reprehensible as female sexual abuse, so all survivors are welcome to read and benefit from this book.

PART ONE

CHAPTER 1

Is There a Hell, or Are We Already In It?

—Spoken by a client regarding the sexual abuse in her family

I don't belong anywhere. I don't belong in my own family. At school, I'm scared to talk or look at anyone. If the other kids knew me, they would hate me. The popular girls in my class have fun together. They laugh a lot. I wish I could be one of them, instead of me.

For much of my long life from deep down inside, I felt worthless. I didn't trust myself or anyone else. Whenever I made a mistake, feelings of shame and self-loathing overwhelmed me. If someone mistreated me, it was my fault. I was the only person on earth who felt like this.

As I grew up, I forced myself to make some eye contact because the two kids who didn't do that looked peculiar. I rarely talked. I was a "loner" with a lot of emotional baggage.

My father made declarations like these: "Nobody wants to hear what you have to say," and "You don't know what you're talking about."

My mother claimed, "You don't deserve the air you breathe," and "You never do anything right."

I believed my parents. These statements were self-fulfilling prophecies. They defined me. They contributed to a lifetime of self-doubt. According to my parents, what I did or said was usually wrong. I was the family scapegoat.

My parents praised my sister for her stellar grades in school and her compliance at home. My mother complained in a whiny voice, "Why can't you be more like your sister?"

I hear that, and I shrink inside. When I'm a speck of dirt, my mother will put me out with the trash. I don't want to be more like my sister.

She is three and one-half years older than I am. She gets along better with our mother. My sister is smarter than I am. I'm cuter. No one listens to me. They just tell me what to do.

One day, when I'm five, Daddy and I are alone in the living room. He sits on our green couch and reads the newspaper. He puts it down and says with a sweet smile, "Come over here and sit on my lap." I do it. We play and snuggle. It's fun. I feel special. I love Daddy a lot.

Oh no! His hand is inside my shorts and underwear again. It's moving around. I hate that. I squirm. Daddy is ruining everything.

He says, "Hold still," in a rough voice.

My mother walks into the room. I see her look at the lump of Daddy's hand under my clothes. Good! She will tell him to quit doing that.

Oh! Mommy's eyes look cold. They are popping out of her head. She glares at me.

She shrieks, "You're nasty. You're disgusting. You should be ashamed of yourself. What's the matter with you? You should know better than to sit on his lap."

Mommy yells and snarls like the neighbor's dog. Her face looks all ugly and twisted. That tears me up inside. I didn't do anything. I feel sick in my stomach. I shrink down in my seat.

I already explained to her, I hate when he touches me like that. I want her to stop Daddy from doing that!

My mother says nothing to my father. He just stands there and frowns. I wish he would make Mommy stop yelling at me.

Finally, it was quiet. My parents slipped away in different directions. I was dying for someone to notice me and hold me and comfort me. I thought they would refuse if I asked.

The next day my parents looked perturbed, with stern faces and wrinkled foreheads. My father informed me we'd have a meeting the following day in his office. When I asked why he looked away and said they'd tell me tomorrow. I was still desperate to hear some kind words. My stomach churned.

My father was a medical doctor. His office and our living space occupied the same building in a residential neighborhood on the edge of a medium-sized Midwestern industrial city. Two large churches next door served as buffers

3

between our place and the busy main street. Streetcars rattled their way on tracks to and from downtown.

His office space used most of the first floor. While shut off from the office area, our kitchen and dining room downstairs were connected by back and front stairs to the bedrooms and living room on the second floor. Just inside the front door was a winding staircase. One time, a visiting child took a forbidden slide down the shiny wood banister. He landed on the first floor in seconds.

Halfway up the stairs was a landing. The previous year, when I was four years old, two older boys trapped me in the closet on that landing. Our parents had told the brothers they were in charge and left the house. The boys coaxed me into the closet to play. They closed the door and turned on the light.

The older boy orders me, "Take off your shorts. Take off your underpants. Your sister refused, so you have to do it." My sister is nowhere in sight. I do what he says. I stand while the boys sit on the floor of the closet. They stare at my bare bottom. I hate it. I feel weak and start to shake.

One of them says, "Turn around. Turn around again."

My body feels stuck, but I do it.

The older boy points his finger at me. "You're a bad girl. If you tell your parents about this, we'll tell them you pulled down your pants."

I felt so ashamed. From then on, no matter what age I was, I wanted to hide from the *piercing male gaze.*

In the office treatment room where that meeting would take place, one wall consisted of pretty, white French doors. They led outside to my father's rose garden. The French doors were a reminder of the elegance of the original house before that room became part of the office.

I always focused on those French doors to hold myself together during the times my father brought me in here. As I know now, he took advantage of his profession, my mother's negligence, and my innocence. He sexually abused me, making the excuse that I had some medical problem.

Ordinarily, in this room patients' injuries and mine were carefully disinfected and bandaged. On this meeting day, the opposite was about to happen—emotional wounds would be inflicted and left to fester. I would "catch" from my parents more of that sickening feeling with the strange smell. I believe now, as an adult, that smell was their sexual shame.

On the meeting day, bright sunlight peeks in around the edges of the blinds on the French doors. I usually feel nervous in here with my father. This time I'm so afraid, my stomach is burning up. I'm weak and shaky. I want to run away. Even though the bottle is closed, the disinfectant smell leaks out. It smells nasty. I can taste it in my mouth.

I watch Daddy's face. It's not friendly. He brings in a chair for my mother. He tells me to sit at the end of the treatment table near him. My legs dangle over the edge. A bright light on a cord hangs near my head.

This is creepy. I never get my parents attention all to myself. Where's my sister? Mommy and I sit while Daddy stands. He's very tall. He's no longer my scary father—he's a scarier doctor wearing a white coat.

Daddy comes closer. His eyes look at the top of my head. He says these words that stick in my brain forever.

"What your mother saw us doing is your fault. Little girls should not bat their eyelashes at their fathers or other men. That can make them lose control. Men can't be expected to control themselves."

What is he talking about? I've done something terrible. My heart beats fast. My stomach turns upside down. My mother nods her head and looks at her lap. She won't look at me. Help!

I don't understand. I want to cry. Daddy says I have control over grown-up men. I know I don't have control over anything. My father is the boss. He says it's my fault. My mother agrees with him. I'm all alone in the world.

When I look back at this ambush, I doubt that I flirted, although it's normal for little girls to flirt with their fathers. Either way that is not a license, an invitation, or an excuse for anyone to sexually abuse a child, no matter what she says or does.

Did my father blame me so my mother wouldn't blame him? Did he try to shame me so I wouldn't tell anyone what he was doing to me? Couldn't he notice the difference between little girls and women? Whatever the diagnosis, the doctor was sick and didn't seem to know it.

As a result of those events, I acquired and retained overwhelming feelings of shame and worthlessness. They lodged in my body, brain, and broken spirit. Unconsciously, from that time forward, I assumed all sexual abuse perpetrated against me—past, present, and future—was automatically my fault. I didn't question that conclusion for decades. For many years I suffered flashbacks from the events I just described. Feelings of abandonment and terror would be triggered by something that happened in the present. I would feel like the scared, lonely child I was back then while trying to live my current older child or adult life. This confusing state could last a few minutes and linger for a few days.

This particular flashback haunted me during my divorce many years later, when I felt all alone in the world again. Of course, then I had no idea where it came from. Flashbacks made me feel crazy until I knew what they were and that other survivors have them, too.

As you would expect, my father was an intelligent, educated person. He was a practicing physician. He had all the prestige, authority, and in his case arrogance which went along with his title. Both my father and my mother had a history of childhood sexual abuse. I'll tell you about that later.

My mother should have known better, too. She had an adequate brain, but no mind of her own. Apparently, my mother's childhood sexual abuse and her dependence on my father blinded her. She was gullible where my father was concerned, awed by his status, and afraid of his anger.

If she believed him, she could deny the incest in our family. She wouldn't need to listen to me.

In that meeting, when my father said I flirted with him, he compared me to my mother's cousin. I'll call her Isabelle. My father made fun of Isabelle to the family and pretended to disapprove of her flirting, yet he was the one who flirted with her when they visited us.

I guess you could say Isabelle was glamorous. I think she was trying to be. Her hair was dyed bright red. Her clothing revealed what was underneath it—much more than my mother's. Her husband, Frank, was tall and thin. His arms and legs seemed uncoordinated with the rest of him. Those appendages were floppy and appeared to have a mind of their own.

I didn't pay much attention to how people looked or what they said back then. I looked at their faces and bodies to determine if I was safe in their presence. That was all I wanted to know.

On one Sunday visit by Isabelle and Frank when I was five years old, my mother was in the kitchen preparing dinner. My sister was away somewhere. Daddy, Cousin Frank and I were sitting in the living room waiting to eat.

Isabelle paused in the doorway for a moment. When she sauntered into the room, the backs of her fancy high heels went slap, slap, slap against her bare feet with every step. Isabelle flipped her long hair over her shoulder. She swung her hips as she moved. You might think she was doing the cha-cha.

My father watches Isabelle. His eyes are Christmas lights—the ones that twinkle. She and my father laugh and tell jokes I don't understand. A strange feeling is in the air. I guess they are flirting. I never did anything like that. I'm only a child.

Although Frank didn't appear to notice them, he soon found a way to retaliate for my father's part in this drama. But first, we sat together at the dining room table for dinner. The highlight of this meal was a medium-rare prime rib roast. Its marvelous aroma drifted throughout the house and office for hours before we could eat. I couldn't tolerate the wait. I loved the crunchy brown potatoes my mother roasted in the pan juices with the meat. Sometimes they were so crunchy/hard they could hurt my mouth when I chewed. We would have a green vegetable and a homemade dessert with that. This meal was my favorite. My mother was an excellent cook.

I remember that nobody criticized me as they usually did while we ate, because we had company. But the main reason I remember this story is that someone tricked my father—and lived.

About an hour after dinner, Cousin Frank asked me to help him find my father. We discovered him in his office, sleeping contentedly while gently snoring. He was lying on the treatment table that he used for patients with back pain. When this table was turned off, it was flat. When turned on, a jumbo-sized roller rose up out of its bed to roll back and forth under the patient's back.

Frank had seen this table in action. He asked me if I knew the location of the switch. I was proud I could show him. Then Frank walked over to the table and flipped the switch.

I didn't expect him to use it! Doesn't Frank know my father has a terrible temper? I freeze. I hold my breath. I watch that big roller moving toward my sleeping father. My heart thumps hard in my chest.

Wham! My father jumps up to his feet and yells, "*&^%#$^%*/! What's happening?"

I know my father will explode because he does that when he's not in control. He'll figure out I told Frank where the switch is. He'll be mad and will say this is my fault.

It's quiet. I can't believe it. My father's face is red. His eyes are bulging. I've never seen this before. He's not yelling. Why is that? Does he only yell at women and children?

Frank sheepishly admitted his guilt. I didn't hear anyone talk about this afterward. A new elephant was added to our herd of elephants in the living room.

After the fateful meeting, when my father blamed me for his abuse, I became more self-conscious. I worried that I was provocative. I tried to be sure I wasn't flirting in some way I didn't recognize. In my body unconsciously, I pulled things in and tightened them up. I was quietly terrified. I tried to be invisible. I hoped, now, my father would stop doing that to me.

A few days later, my father probably told my mother he was going to tuck me in as he often did. When he arrived at my room, I pretended I was asleep. I was wide awake and frozen to the spot.

Some part of me watches from a place on the ceiling. From up there, it looks like this is happening to some other little girl, but I have all the icky feelings inside me. I hate the place he touches. I hate myself.

Usually, he doesn't talk. This time, my father says in a stern voice, "Your mother is already sick. If you tell her what we're doing, it will kill her."

I don't want that! No matter what Daddy does, I can never tell my mother again.

After my father leaves, I remember his words. I'm so scared, I hurry to the bathroom to throw up. He hears me. I think Daddy will be mad at me, but he's a little bit nice for a moment before he disappears.

As usual, during the next few days after my father sexually abused me, he avoided me. Each time he did that, I felt rejected and crazy. I felt confused, too—closely connected to him and disconnected at the same time. Since my father pretended everything was normal, as if this had never happened, I doubted my perception. I felt crazy. I wondered if I imagined this abuse. I didn't.

Some part of me recalled some piece of most abuse events. It could be a picture in my mind or a particular smell. It could be a feeling, some words or a strange aversion to something ordinary, like eating a banana out of the skin. I avoided eating bananas that way for years before I realized it reminded me of particular events I wanted to forget.

My bedroom was located down the hall and around the corner from the other two bedrooms. Then you had to walk through another room to get to mine. To say I felt isolated is putting it mildly. I don't know how they heard me cry when I was a baby.

My mother explained later that she didn't want to upset my sister by moving her out of the bedroom next door to my parents' room. She said she didn't want to cause sibling rivalry. She made it easy for my father to abuse me in privacy.

Every night when I go to bed, I lie there and listen for my father's footsteps coming down the hall. I'm scared. I shiver. My muscles are tight. I want to hide, but I know he would find me.

When I wait, and I wait, and I don't hear him, I calm down some. Occasionally, I feel sad when he doesn't come. In a way, sometimes I want his abuse even though I hate it. I need attention badly.

Sometimes I knew and sometimes I didn't know what my father did to me. I forgot or buried the memories. It was like this: when sexual abuse was happening, I knew it was happening to some extent. When it wasn't happening, I wasn't always aware that it had happened, but I felt the accompanying feelings of shame, helplessness, and despair.

I did know I felt utterly dominated by my father. Sometimes he "played" with me and gave me sloppy, noisy kisses in front of my mother. I hated the slobbery wetness and the disgusting noise he made with his mouth. I felt sick to my stomach. My mother watched that and said nothing.

When I told my father I didn't want him to do that kissing thing, he was offended. He thought it was cute and said, "You're no fun." That became another self-fulfilling prophecy which I believed.

If my father saw me bend over, he'd say my back end was a target. "Ha, ha, ha." He would walk into our only bathroom without warning. When I asked him to knock first, he refused, declaring, "I'm the head of the household. I can do anything I want." My mother enabled my father; even though I pleaded with her, she insisted I couldn't use the bathroom lock because I might get locked in. I felt defenseless. I dreaded using the bathroom when he was nearby.

I never expected to have a future. Unconsciously, I feared my father's abuse would worsen. He would kill me with his size and power.

I don't know what I feel most of the time. I know I never feel safe or in charge of my own body. I try not to feel anything because I'm not allowed to show it or talk about it. My parents made that rule, even though they don't follow it themselves.

Several other people molested me when I was little. Two were friends of the family, and two were female babysitters. Apparently, potential sex abusers could just look at me and see I had lost my power. Unconsciously, I concluded abuse happened to me because I was unworthy of any other kind of treatment.

If those abusers didn't care what I wanted, that was nothing new. I froze and dissociated. (Dissociation means feeling disconnected from memory, identity, and body.) Those abusers left scars. I say more about my father's abuse in Chapter 2, and in Chapter 5, I explain how I learned some of those abuse details.

From age two months to thirteen years, my father sexually abused me in a variety of ways, including rape, at a variety of times and places. I never knew what to expect or when to expect it. I was scared stiff. My brain was on alert 24/7.

This is incest. I hate that word. Incest. I wrote much of this book before I dared to write that word. When I did, it was no accident; it was a hit and run. Incest. I hate that it happened to me. I'm angry right now as I consider what that word means.

Incest refers to an older male or female family member, relative, or close friend who sexually preys on a younger family member. Incest perpetrators differ from pedophiles because their abuse is usually restricted to family members or close family friends. Incest is deceitful and incredibly harmful. It can wreck lives. I believe it ruined my mother. I know it sabotaged the positive feelings I could have had about myself and my body. Incest destroyed my ability to love and trust other people.

Multiple incest events usually involve painful emotional neglect, as well. Often, someone other than the abuser is not paying attention to what is happening to the child, is in denial, or is enabling the abuser.

If you live with the perpetrator, you are always a target. You never know when he or she will creep into your room to molest you or worse. If the perpetrator comes to your house to visit, his/her visits are unbearable. You pretend everything is fine. You try to avoid him without making a scene. You know if you tell someone, it might create another set of problems.

My parents were mostly of German descent. I had two sets of grandparents and a few aunts, uncles and cousins from both sides of the family. We saw them infrequently when I was young and seldom or never after that. It seemed like my parents didn't want to be with them. We visited my father's parents when we took a vacation. My mother's cousin Isabelle and her husband, whom I mentioned earlier, were the relatives we saw the most, but even those visits were infrequent.

I remember overhearing visiting relatives or friends question my father about me. I don't know if this was out of concern, or if they were making small talk. I heard the end of more than one conversation in which my father said, "Something is wrong with that girl."

Why don't you tell them what it is, Daddy?

Now, when I look at my old family pictures, it's clear that I look tense and somber. One of the rules in our family was *Don't Talk*, and I didn't. I was close to no one and too scared and ashamed to reach out.

I can't help wondering: What if just one adult had said to me, "Your parents are wrong. Don't believe them. They abuse you, and it's not your fault." Could I have avoided picking up my parents' blame, pain, and negativity, and would I have stopped believing everything they told me?

Fortunately for me, my dysfunctional family was free of some of the significant sources of trauma which are experienced by many sex abuse survivors. Those include poverty, domestic violence, brutal physical abuse, and divorced or incarcerated parents. Home life, for me, could have been much worse.

My parents provided me with good food, clothing, shelter, excellent schools, and college education. I belonged to upper-middle-class white America. I could see the majority in action—how things were done, what was expected, who was accepted, etc. That was the only group to which I felt I belonged.

I was painfully uncertain about what was real and who was right in my family. Different realities coexisted in my head. From the outside, we looked like a conventional upper-middle-class family. Apparently, we were very convincing. People treated us with respect and sometimes envy. Our affluence was a vital part of the abuse cover-up. It seemed to convince others we were successful in every way. Knowing we looked good was confusing to me. I sure didn't feel good. Inside the family, my mother, father, and sister played their "perfect family" roles. See the pretty, tidy, big house and the excellent table manners when they eat a good dinner together every night: My mother, the ill/self-sacrificing near-saint; my father, the dedicated doctor/great provider; and my sister, the perfect student/obedient daughter. Then there was me. I was not a part of those lovely family dinners for my first six years. I'll tell you about that later.

Today, I know my dysfunctional family members lied, denied, and pretended to themselves and each other about many issues. I did that too. By day, I pretended everything was fine. I went through the motions of living. Then I survived those nights when my father molested me or whatever he did. I had usually repressed what happened by the next day. Then I dragged myself to school, well-dressed, to be sure, with no visible wounds.

Until recently, I thought my father was my biggest problem. My mother seemed so helpless and innocent, but now I realize she bashed me and undermined me regularly. I could not feel any warmth from her toward me.

REFLECTIONS

This first chapter tells the story of how I became a shameful, self-loathing little person. Eventually, I rescued myself with invaluable help from other sources. Over time, I became a contented, caring, and happy person. This is the account of what I did to achieve that. Please hang in there with me if you can. It gets a lot better.

An explanation of terms and concepts is in the Glossary

CHAPTER 2

Family Portrait

Mommy hates me. I feel it every day, but I don't let myself believe it. She only looks at me or talks to me when she wants to "correct" me. She doesn't act glad to see me when I come home. If Mommy and I are together, and Daddy or my sister walks into the room, her eyes light up. She goes from sad to happy. She forgets I'm there.

If I told this to my family, they'd say, "Don't be silly."

I worry when I hear people say, "If your own mother doesn't like you, who will?"

I told Mommy several times that I can't stand the way Daddy touches me down there. I know she saw him do it, but she turns to ice, and says, "Don't talk about your father that way," or 'He wouldn't do that," or "You were asking for it."

Her answers make me feel like I'm nuts.

Sometimes Daddy tells Mommy, "You don't pay any attention to her."

One time while I hear that, I'm sitting alone in the living room on their precious antique sofa. I'm glad my father knows I'm lonely and tries to help me.

She insists, "I do pay attention to her. You're not around here enough to see it."

I say to myself, "Mommy tells me not to lie, but she does it."

When they talk about me, why do they call me "her" instead of my name?

As for our antique furniture, we had a houseful. My mother's favorite antique was the cobbler's bench. If I got too close, I could smell the musty wood compartments that held the cobbler's tools. The leather on the seat where the cobblers sat was faded brown with cracks. What's so special about it?

My parents loved antiques—patinas and three-faced glass. I was jealous. These objects received a lot of attention, while I got so little, especially from my mother. This is the kind of attention she gave me: "Be careful of that weak chair leg. Don't lean on that table. Don't spill that drink. You know these pieces are valuable." Her animosity hurt.

Although I cringed at the sound of her voice, I knew my mother looked good—she wouldn't have been caught dead looking anything but good. Every day she put on lipstick and combed her hair again just before she expected my father to return.

She was slim, pretty, and short. When my mother and my tall father stood next to each other, they looked mismatched. The top of her head didn't reach his shoulder. Her brown hair had a pretty silver streak next to her face. She explained the streak turned to silver when she was in college and never changed back.

When my mother didn't ignore me, and I talked about my activities, she would explain in great detail how what I did, or wanted to do, would lead to catastrophe. She squelched my ideas. Then I would doubt my judgment.

When my mother's anger turned to rage, she was a volcanic eruption. If I tried to say something or leave the room, she would start her harangue all over again. Every bit of me was dying to escape, but I had to stay, trapped, and miserable. Most of her complaints were about not doing chores right or on her schedule. I was sluggish about getting ready for school. I didn't like it. Sometimes my body refused to move. She went overboard with intensity—I was usually guilty as charged.

My father and sister say I must do everything I can to help Mommy. She's weak from her heart trouble. But I need help, too. I'm the littlest. I'm way behind everybody.

Mommy won't stick up for me with my father. She loves my sister lots more than me. If she gave me some love, I would have something inside to give back to her.

I'm dying for Mommy to look at me when she's not mad, listen to me and care about me. It would only take a little bit of her energy. I would love to feel I belong to her and this family.

When I'm six years old, Mommy wants to have a talk. This is the worst one ever. She complains about problems that aren't even about me. She gripes about her life and the work she has to do. I know being sick makes everything harder for her, but why is she blaming me? She yells, "You didn't do this. You didn't do that. Your room isn't clean enough. Do it again." Her guilt trips make me feel like crap.

I don't know how we got to this place, but then Mommy, with the meanest look I ever saw on her face, says, "I'd like to break your neck" and "Look at me when I'm talking to you," one right after the other.

She usually doesn't hit me, but she slaps my face when I tell her, "I don't want to look at you." She says, "I don't love you now, and I never did. I hate you."

I've heard her say some of this before. It breaks my heart again. If I speak another word, this will get worse. I feel beat up. I feel helpless, but I'm mad too. My stomach is going to burst. I put my hands on it to hold it in.

I want to shove her down the basement stairs. I picture her with a pile of dirty laundry tumbling down those steep steps. Clothes fall everywhere. But then I think of Mommy's weak heart, and I realize how much it would hurt her if I pushed her. In my mind, I see her lying on that hard concrete floor. My body fills up with the worst possible guilty feelings. I slump in my chair and put my head in my hands.

When I first wrote this memory here, I stated that I hoped my mother would *accidentally* fall—but then my breath caught in my throat and I realized that wasn't the truth. I had wanted to *push* her and felt I could easily do it. No wonder I inflicted such a harsh sentence on myself. Following this event, for many years when something undesirable happened to me, the little voice in my head said, "Good, you deserve it," just like my mother would tell me. She said I never did anything right. My mother was impossible to please. I stopped thinking for myself, but I gave my mother resistance in return. If I couldn't get positive feedback from her, I could get the other kind.

My feelings about Mommy are so messed up. Occasionally, I feel a little love for her. I'm supposed to have a lot more love for my mother like my sister does. I feel sorry for her a lot. I feel her painful feelings. I'm scared when my father yells at her. Mommy is alone a lot and doesn't do much. Sometimes she takes the streetcar downtown to shop. I go with her if she has no one to watch me. It's not fun.

Often my mother seemed fragile like one of her special antiques. That's how other people saw her. She was fearful of driving a car, being struck by lightning, or attacked by robbers and rapists. I think she blamed me and her heart disease for the problems in her life. My mother didn't talk about her real feelings, but I know, now, she felt anxious and depressed most of the time. When I look back, she seems very childlike. She must have had many wounds to her heart and soul with no chance to heal them.

Anything to do with the toilet or sex is "disgusting and too nasty to talk about." Mommy wrinkles her nose and shakes her head. She warns my sister and me that we might be attacked by strangers when we leave the house if we aren't careful. How are we supposed to be careful?

To deny her emotional neglect and fit into the family, most of the time I believed the family myth: My mother was a hardworking, loving, self-sacrificing parent to both daughters.

As an adult, I was out of touch with myself but not with that mother myth. When I was pregnant with my daughter, my husband and I planned to honor my deceased mother by giving our baby girl her name. It seemed like a good idea; everyone would approve. Fortunately, before our daughter was born, I began to see the flaws in that myth. I didn't explain to my sister why I changed my mind—it seemed she had no idea what it was like for me in that family. Later, my sister named her own newborn daughter after our mother. We were both satisfied with that decision.

There was one tiny exception to my negative experience of my mother. Occasionally, for some reason, my mother liked to eat popcorn with me. It may have been because my father and sister didn't like popcorn, or maybe she just wanted someone else to make it for her.

After I made the popcorn, we would sit down together, eat, and talk. I should say my mother talked, but she spoke to me. She wanted me. We ate the popcorn with milk as you do cereal. Most people think this sounds disgusting, but it was delicious.

As I'm writing and remembering these times, formerly imprisoned tears escape their little cells. They slide down my cheeks. Can you believe popcorn is still my favorite food? It's my number one comfort food. Just now I realize this "tiny exception" isn't tiny. That ritual must have given me something to hold on to in the past. It's okay with me if it still does, even though part of me says, "That's pathetic."

I have a picture of my mother, which I like a lot. She's standing outside in the wind holding her hat on her head. With her little smile, she's cute and appealing. She looks like someone I'd like to know.

When I was dating my first husband, we spent a day at my parents' house, where he met my mother. Afterward, I asked him, "What did you think of her?"

Joe said, "Well, it was strange. Your mother didn't act like a mother."

"What did she act like?"

"Well, maybe like a sister—but not that, either. Like not involved in your life." I was puzzled. I didn't recognize how accurate Joe's observation was until later. Soon after that, my mother died unexpectedly from an aneurysm. My father, sister, and I sat in the hospital waiting room just before she passed. She wanted to see my father, then my sister, then my father again. My mother said goodbye to them. She said nothing to me. At that time, I was still in denial of her real feelings about me. I chose not to notice her final rejection.

Now, I maintain, since she was in the hospital dying anyway, it wouldn't have killed her to leave me with a kind thought. Anything like "Have a good life" would have been beautiful to hear.

A couple of months after my mother's death, as I was shopping for boots, I debated with myself about what my mother would want me to choose. And then it hit me. *I'm still trying to please her, but she's gone!* She's finally off my back. I felt a rush of relief. I grieved, not much for her, but for the loving mother-daughter relationship I never experienced.

My father quickly remarried. My new middle-aged stepmother was beautiful and always perfectly dressed. She was tall like my father. They were a stunning couple when they stood next to each other. They must have planned that.

My sister and I were unhappy to learn they had been having an affair while our mother was alive. We were grown up and didn't need a new mother and two new step-siblings. But our stepmother met our displeasure with kindness. She was the only one who wanted us to be a family. Later, what blending of the family there was fell apart when she died.

Once my stepmother started talking, she couldn't, or wouldn't stop. (Good Grief! I just realized that's how my mother was when she was angry.) This stepmother's habit, although annoying, became an advantage in the following situation.

During our first visit after they married, my stepmother took my first husband for a ride in the new car my father had given her. My stepmother hadn't learned the family rules yet, such as, "Never talk about the family." She told my first husband the family secrets my father had recently divulged to her when he broke his own rule.

She and my first husband were away for a long time. I think my father feared that some infidelity (other than his own) was taking place. He glared at his new wife when they returned and said sharply, "%^$#*$&*#! We are married. I expect you to act like it. I expect you to know when to come home."

Later, when we were alone, my first husband repeated what my stepmother had told him. I stored this information somewhere in my brain until I started writing this book. The following is my father's own story about what transpired at the time of my birth, as told by my stepmother to my first husband. My father informed my mother he planned to leave her for another woman. My mother felt "ugly and misshapen" and unable to compete *because she was pregnant with me.* At that time, cultural norms dictated that women should hide the baby bulge. It was considered unattractive, especially to men.

My mother had already lost my father emotionally. She was brokenhearted at the prospect of losing him altogether. She didn't want a second child, especially one conceived while her husband was cheating.

Recently, I was shocked at the following revelation: Early in my mother's pregnancy with me, my parents tried to illegally abort me in my father's medical office. In fact, they attempted abortion three separate times. My father was unsuccessful with each abortion effort. That would be unusual for him. Failure was the last thing he was willing to allow or admit.

I felt stunned and violated when I heard this. I had often worried that I exaggerated how insensitive my parents were. I saw now they were more coldhearted and self-centered than I ever imagined.

So this is how I started my life—my father repeatedly trying to snag me, or whatever they do, out of my mother's womb? That is supposed to be the safest place there is. A big lump developed in my throat and another one in my gut. I said some kind words to that unborn inner child.

These abortion attempts took place before the use of ultrasound for determining gender. If my father wished to keep me, in case I was the boy he wanted, and he could tolerate saying he failed with the abortions, my father could have it both ways. My mother would stop complaining, and he would have a chance for a son. My birth as a girl was a unanimous disappointment.

Although I felt sick and angry about this information, again, I felt validated. My perceptions were accurate. My feelings were appropriate. Now my parents' negative attitudes and opinions which I carried around in my head started to fade into the distance behind me. I'm right about them, more or less. I felt a lot of relief.

My sister was born into happier times, more than three years before me. That was before the relationship between my parents went sour. She found a foothold in my mother's cold heart.

That sarcasm must mean I have something to work on. Did I say I was jealous of my sister? I didn't? I was seriously jealous of my sister. My mother and sister were the only members of the family who were anything like close to each other.

After school, my sister often went into our parents' bedroom to talk to my mother during my mother's rest periods. I think my mother called them rest periods so she could visit with my sister, but not me. They closed the door. I pretended I didn't care, but it hurt so much to feel left out. At the same time, my father was behind closed doors, too—in his office, meeting with his patients or whatever he did in there. (Sometimes there was hanky-panky with a secretary. As a child, I didn't know that yet.) I was not allowed to disturb him unless the building was going up in flames. There was no one to say, "Hello, how was your day?" On rare occasions, my mother appeared and gave us cookies and milk after school.

I think my sister is better than I am because my mother likes her so much more.

My sister was tall. Her hair was straight and manageable. She rolled it up in rags or curlers at night to create a "page boy" hairdo that turned under at the ends. Her hair was neat and tidy, unlike mine, which was wild and curly. I couldn't stand my own hair until I started to like myself.

My mother says my sister is shy. Maybe she is, but her shyness is nothing compared to mine. My sister has friends who know her. I don't know who my sister is or what she thinks. I don't have any friends most of the time. I don't talk to anyone.

My sister won't play with me or help me do or learn anything. She says I should just do what my mother wants. She blames me for our mother being upset. My sister ignores me worse than my mother does.

Sometimes I hear my mother tell her, "I can't stand your sister. She won't help. She never does what she's told. She never does anything right." I feel sick and sad, and like a terrible person, when I hear that.

One time when I was in kindergarten, I remember walking home from school with my sister and her friends. It was a warm, rainy day but not raining at the time. Suddenly my panties fell down onto the sidewalk. I stood still, in confusion, the panties looped around my ankles. The elastic around the top had failed. That morning, I had forgotten to pin the top edges together to make it narrower as I usually did. (I rarely asked for help.)

My frantic sister ordered me to step out of the offending panties. She scooped them up as fast as she could and dropped them inside the collapsed, blue-striped umbrella she was carrying. She was so quick, nobody noticed. That was possibly the first, but certainly the last, time we walked home from school together.

My sister told that story, in a disdainful voice, to my parents during dinner that evening. I was a huge embarrassment to her. Her focus was on saving face. She had to look good. I was the screw-up. This story became one of those big family jokes.

In her defense, my sister was taught to "look good." She wasn't told to take care of her little sister. She didn't see anyone else doing it, so why would she? She was invested in taking care of our mother.

When the time came, my mother convinced my father to pay tuition to a private high school for my sister. Then my mother found special activities for her to learn so she could be "well-rounded." Sometimes I was an add-on, like with the music and the swimming lessons. My sister and I had the same music teacher. He knew how to play and teach her instrument, but admitted he only was guessing with mine.

In the swimming pool, my sister was tall enough, but I was too short to stand in the shallow end and breathe while the teacher talked. I stood on my tiptoes. I stretched up as high as possible, so I didn't choke on the water splashing into my mouth. Nobody took my difficulties seriously.

The following is my theory about my mother's very different relationships with her two daughters. My sister's life was the life my mother missed because of her sexual abuse and heart disease. My mother could live my sister's life, vicariously, if she shaped it in a certain way. My life was the one my mother had suffered through as a child and wanted to reject, through rejecting me—after she dumped her painful feelings onto me.

While writing about my mother, I began to feel guilty. Was I whining and complaining like she did? Wasn't I different from her? Were my complaints more legitimate than hers? I didn't know. I was suspicious of myself.

I have discovered I was very much like my mother. I resisted believing that, but I had to accept it when I saw it. In many ways, I was more like my mother than my sister was. How could that have happened? I never wanted to be like her.

The truth was, I could be intensely angry, cynical, bossy, controlling, and critical, too. My mother's role modeling was influential then, but I'm responsible for who I am now. I've done a lot of work on my attitude, and I still do. To separate myself from my mother, be different, and find the love in me—that was and is my challenge.

During most of my therapy, it was no accident that I avoided working on that buried mother pain. I was afraid of its depth and intensity. My last therapist was a kind, wise, older woman with a rich Latvian accent. If I had been born to a mother like her, I wouldn't have needed her services. (Sadly, though, this therapist wouldn't let me take her home and keep her.) I tried to be fair in talking to her about my mother and me. After she listened, my therapist described her well: "Your mother was a very sick 'voman.'" That was some help, but she declined to elaborate. Later, I repeated this comment, complete with her Latvian accent, to my second husband. We enjoyed a hearty laugh. Her response sounded unprofessional but accurate.

What did I learn from my mother about relationships with women? They won't like me. They will criticize, neglect, and abandon me as my mother did. I needed women friends, and I needed a mother even more. I couldn't reach out for either one.

Years earlier—long before I admitted to myself that my mother's betrayal was equally damaging—I had gone to therapy to cope with the effects of my father's sexual abuse. I was so intimidated by him, I imagined any minute my father would burst through the door and snatch me out of the therapy room. I was talking about him. I was violating his rules.

So many sessions spent on my father. So many filled with anger, rage, and hurt. Eventually, I grew sick of talking about him, but I can take another look at him now.

My father was the central figure in the family for my entire childhood. He was prominent in my mind for most of my adult life. As the strongest, loudest, scariest most demanding member of the family, he was larger than life. I envied his power. I despised how he used it.

He determined what we would all do—how, when, where. He was the sole wage earner. He alone could decide how to spend money. My father could be stingy and manipulative about sharing it. Who else could you ask the third time for your allowance, then watch him take six agonizing minutes putting his right hand in the pocket where he kept the dollars and bringing it out with no money in it—over and over? I would wait and watch the hand while he talked about something else. Sometimes I would give up and walk away. But then I had to try again.

If I asked my mother for money, she would automatically say, "We can't afford it." I had a lifelong allergy to asking anyone to give me money.

People commented on my father's good looks. He was unusually handsome—tall and slim with bushy hair and eyebrows. His dark, penetrating eyes stood out the most, after his warm laugh. He could laugh at anything, and it would sound good. He had great charisma. He could make socially uncomfortable people feel comfortable. When I was little, I loved him a lot. His smile would make me happy. I was hungry for his scarce approval.

My father had an excellent bedside manner with his patients. When his office was part of our house, sometimes I heard, not the words, but the tone of his voice from upstairs in my bedroom. He sounded so kind, so soothing. He was so interested in what they had to say. It caused me excruciating pain as a child to hear that.

Why doesn't my father speak to me that way? And listen?
When I try to talk to him, he looks like he can't wait to get away. I
tell myself, "Get the words out quickly before he looks for his next
thing or leaves the room." I hate feeling so unimportant.

We never had a father-daughter talk—not when I had
my first date, not when I went off to college, not when I got
married. I blamed myself for not being enough. Just now, it
occurs to me my father was probably afraid I would bring
up his awful abuse, and he would be the one trapped, for
a change. We never talked about that. How incredibly sad
that he made that choice.

When a patient told stories of childhood sexual abuse, did
my father squirm? What did he say? Was he inappropriate
with any of his patients? He had the opportunity, and he
had excuse skills.

As an adult, when I finally recognized my first husband
had a drinking problem, I realized my father did too. This
shouldn't have been too tricky to determine for either of them,
but I had mastered the arts of denial and codependency. Both
of them appeared to manage their drinking reasonably well,
but it affected and infected both my childhood and adult
families. Their use showed up in poor behavior and attitudes,
but especially in my father's sudden hot temper tantrums.
They scared the heck out of me.

My father could be a Jekyll and Hyde—happy one moment
and in a rage the next. I taught myself, as a child, not to
enjoy the fun part. I needed to be mentally on guard for the

explosion, in case there was one. This was unfortunate because my father was the only one in the family who played or laughed or tried to make jokes. I say *tried* because sometimes he teased me and it wasn't funny.

My father refused to be accountable for his behavior. If I suggested I didn't like something he did, I would regret it. He would become angry and swear loudly. He turned it around and blamed me. More anger and the silent treatment would follow. It wasn't worth it to tangle with him. I could see my mother was hurt by that, sometimes. She protected him and excused his behavior.

I never confronted my father about his sexual abuse. I was sure it would end badly with no benefit to me. I was sure he would never admit it. He had too much to lose and I had no one to back me up. I was too scared, anyway. I'll never know for sure what would have happened.

When my father sexually abused me, he seemed spacy and disconnected from himself and from me. His eyes had a glazed look. That intensified my feelings of being abandoned and unloved. I know now, from my own experience, that he was dissociating most of the time. I could feel my father's lust and his need for complete control. He told me what to do. I did it. Protesting didn't help.

He first molested me when I was two months old. (I'll tell you how I know that in Chapter 5.) He did things to me that I didn't want and forced me to do things to him that I didn't want to do—in my bed, in his office, in the car (rarely), and while giving me the spankings my mother requested. As I said earlier, he performed what he claimed were necessary medical procedures and enemas, which I realize now were excuses for abuse and penetration. My father's lust was apparent during all these activities. I could see it in the look on his face and sense it in the feel and smell in the air. That added to my pain. I felt humiliated, degraded, and betrayed.

As an adult, I discovered inappropriate baby pictures he had photographed and developed himself. I felt a rush of shame and overwhelm as if I had just done something terribly wrong. I think he belonged to some kind of group that shared these pictures.

At age eleven, I remember feeling exposed and humiliated while lying naked on my father's treatment table when my mother walked into the room. (I don't recall what happened before she arrived.) He quickly told her that something was wrong with my physical development and that he would treat it.

Later, when he didn't follow up with a plan, I worried. When I asked him about my condition, he walked away, mumbling, "It's nothing." That made me very angry. I had feared something was wrong with my body for no reason. That didn't matter to him.

I am shocked right now to realize how unloving and disrespectful my father's behavior was toward me. He didn't see me as a real person. I didn't feel like a real person. He never wondered or asked what I thought or felt. Sometimes he pretended to care, but it was shallow. He depended on his charisma, which was backed up by nothing, apparently. I was supposed to be thrilled about what he gave me for Christmas. Whatever it was, it wasn't what I wanted or needed from him.

My father demanded the worst when I was twelve and thirteen years old. Each time, I was terrified and frozen in the fight/flight/freeze response. Each time, he was disappointed with me. I was "supposed to move around" and act as if I liked it. I guess he expected me to behave like a consenting woman. I felt terribly guilty for failing him. I don't know what was wrong with him, sexually, that he blamed on me. So much manipulation and deception. So little love.

There was another side to my relationship with my father. When he was playful and fun, I felt good about myself. When I was physically hurt or sick, my father was usually gentle and helpful. He applied bandaids deftly, with appropriate concern for the pain. I wanted to be a patient and receive that kind of attention. I wonder if that explains why I caught the majority of childhood communicable diseases in spite of the shots. He was the first man to whom I was addicted, just as my mother had been since long before me.

My father showed his tender side to his roses. He grew the biggest and best roses he could find. He tended them lovingly. Sometimes he brought a few of the perfect ones inside for my mother to admire. He was as eager for praise as a five-year-old.

I was surprised to see the depth of his vulnerability at those times. I could see the extent of his woundedness too. Ordinarily, both were carefully hidden. No one other than my father was allowed into that rose garden or the garden of his vulnerability. I don't know what else lived and grew there.

My father thought his parenting obligations were strictly financial, which was not unusual during that era. He refused to drive me anywhere during the entire time I lived with him unless it was a rare trip with the family. His excuse was that he might need to make a house call for a patient emergency, although he'd stopped making house calls when I was six years old. Since my mother didn't drive, I would have to ask people for rides, and I was reluctant to request anything from anybody. I became accustomed to staying home.

I had few or no friends and participated in no after school activities. I rarely went anywhere except school and the dime store, until I started to date boys with cars at age sixteen.

When I was eleven, some girls asked me to walk to the movie theatre, nearby, to see a movie. I wanted to go. I begged my father.

He said, "No, it's not safe for you to walk in the dark."

I argued, "It's a safe neighborhood. Please let me go."

"No."

"Will you drive us?"

I already knew the answer. The girls went without me. I stayed home and felt helpless and discouraged. I felt my body and my hope cave in. This didn't bother my mother. She was okay with her decision not to drive.

When my sister was old enough, she took driver's education classes. When I reached the same age, my father wouldn't let me take the classes and he refused to give me one driving lesson. My boyfriend wanted to help. After we finished playing tennis one day, my boyfriend let me drive his car out of the parking lot into traffic. I had the idea we should start with something more manageable, but I didn't speak up. He was doing me a favor.

I put my foot on the gas instead of the brake and immediately smashed into another car. We appeared in court but weren't charged. The woman whose car I'd hit showed up in a neck brace. I felt guilty. I always wondered if she was pretending or if she was really hurt.

My father said the accident was what he would expect from me, and "the boy" should have known better than to let me drive his car. My father refused to pay the insurance deductible for the accident. Even though my boyfriend was stuck with the bill, he continued to like me, but that was the end of the driving lessons.

There was no reason why I couldn't learn to drive. I wasn't stupid or disabled.

If my parents think I'm incapable, why don't they help me do better?

Finally, my first husband taught me to drive at age twenty-two. I had absolutely no confidence. Like my mother, I was scared. My biggest fear was merging onto freeways; I avoided freeway driving for years. Eventually, I taught myself to do it anyway with visualization and desensitization techniques I learned as a counselor. I improved in time, but driving is a metaphor for living. I was afraid of both.

When I was little, I loved my father as much as I feared him. I separated his love from his anger. He was either good or bad, depending on what had just happened. I was confused. Inconsistency was his norm. I didn't figure in the sexual abuse, then.

As I grew older and started to mentally connect it all, including his abuse, I felt disgusted by his presence. I couldn't stand to be touched by him. Occasionally, he would put his arm around me during a rare visit and pretend we had a decent relationship. I cringed. I said nothing. I couldn't escape fast enough.

One time, as an adult, I went home without my husband and children to visit my father. I was in therapy. I had a list of questions about my childhood and a plan for how I wanted to be when I was with him. I didn't intend to confront him about his abuse.

Usually, when I visited, I would slip into a passive role as I did when I lived with my father and mother. I would feel like I did as a child—depressed, needy, flat, and intimidated. My clients have told me of similar experiences. They were capable and confident in the adult world but could go home to abusive parents and feel five years old.

Not me, when I visited this time. As I asked some preliminary questions, my stepmother came from the kitchen. It seemed like she needed to protect someone, or maybe she wanted to learn something. I fished for information. I asked about alcoholism in the family. Of course, he insisted there wasn't any. The other questions I don't remember, except for the important one: "What was wrong with my mother when I was born?"

My father said, "Oh, we wanted you."

That was not an answer to the question. It was not the truth. Family history was locked up tight. At my request, he drove me to my childhood home—the house/office I described in Chapter One. It looked smaller. We stayed outside. It didn't stir up anything in me or tell me what I wanted to know. At that visit, little was accomplished in gaining information, but I was delighted that I could remain my adult self. That was a huge accomplishment.

I grew to dislike my father more and more as I realized how damaged I was. He never abused my children; he didn't even try to charm them. It may be because my stepmother hovered over my children every minute during the once or twice per year that we were together. I don't know what she knew of his history. I followed the rules—I never asked her. I was thoroughly brainwashed, still.

My father committed suicide in his early eighties. He shot himself in the bedroom he shared with my stepmother. I hadn't seen him for two years. Like my mother, he didn't say goodbye. He left me, but not my sister, a small sum of money.

After the shock of his suicide, I fended off a variety of reactions. The angry one I didn't share with anyone was, "You should have told me you wanted to be dead. I would have been glad to shoot you."

Here's what I learned about relationships with men. You must pay a high emotional price to get what you need from a man. Sometimes you get worse than nothing, and sometimes you get more. Then you expect and hope for more, and you get disappointed again with less.

REFLECTIONS

My mother and sister claimed I was stubborn like my father. I was. I'm sure that helped me survive. I'm amazed at the ability of the human spirit—and mine, in particular—to persevere under those conditions.

An explanation of terms and concepts can be found in the Glossary.

CHAPTER 3

The Maid Who Loved Me

My mother knew someone who desperately wanted a baby. My father wouldn't agree to give me away. (She told me this later.) My father persisted in his affair, which continued to devastate my mother. He was willing to hire help for childcare and housework after I was born. Poor black women from the inner city worked these jobs. Some of them could ride the streetcar to our part of town and exit almost at our doorstep.

I have a picture etched in my mind, although I probably couldn't have seen this at birth. My mother is holding me at arm's length as a new baby. I'm wrapped in a white blanket. She hands me to the maid. She says, "Take her," and she never takes me back.

My father fired the first maid when he discovered why his drinks had lost their oomph. She admitted she drank from each of the bottles of gin, bourbon, vodka, etc., and replaced the alcohol with water. I don't know anything about the second maid, but the third one was a gift from the universe. I'll call her Angel.

I remember Angel's appearance, slightly. A terrible accident or physical attack had befallen her before she came to work for us. Broken bones and a lack of medical attention had left her facial features crooked and scarred. In spite of that, Angel's brown face had a sweet, warm expression.

Angel worked hard. She nurtured everyone. She was afraid of my father. Five days per week, Angel did the housekeeping, laundry, ironing, and childcare for me. She pressed my father's patient gowns with a machine called a mangle. I never knew why it was called that. It never mangled them.

Angel had no experience cooking white people's food. My mother said she didn't want to risk my father's displeasure while Angel learned. My mother couldn't admit to liking anything she did herself, but I think she wanted to keep the cooking job.

I stayed around Angel a lot while she worked. I remember playing on the kitchen floor while she washed dishes. I can't remember what she said, but her voice was gentle and soft. Sometimes she murmured to herself. Sometimes she laughed.

My mother told me not to bother Angel too much because Angel had a lot of work to do. Clearly, childcare for me took second place in Angel's job description. My mother spent time in her room with my sister after school, and she cooked dinner. I don't know what else she did. I didn't see my mother much.

Every evening, my mother, father, and sister ate dinner together in the dining room. The maid or my mother fed me first in the kitchen. This arrangement was my mother's idea. She explained it this way: "Babies and little children are messy. They spill things. They disrupt conversations with their crying, irrelevant talking, and poor table manners." Apparently, my older sister never had these problems.

When Angel came to work for us, I was almost three years old. I was still eating in the kitchen in the maid's company. (It was improper for a maid to eat with me, due to the current belief that black people and white people should not mix.) One evening a female relative visited Angel at dinnertime. They shook their heads and *tsked*. They agreed my separation from the family was "a shame."

Sometimes from the kitchen, I could hear my mother talking and fake-laughing. She was pretending everything was perfect with the three of them together in the dining room.

I feel so sad. I feel so left out of my family. I'm no good at all. I don't care if I eat.

My childhood feelings of rejection led to agony for most of my life whenever I was a member of a group. I never felt I belonged.

As I look back, I realize that dinnertime was the only regular opportunity my mother had to spend time with my father. He was usually busy without her. He took a nap right after dinner and saw patients in the evening.

I believe with these dinners for three, my mother tried to recreate the good times she enjoyed with my father and my sister before I was born. Perhaps she hoped to win him back. He hadn't left her for the other woman. Maybe she was jealous of the attention my father gave me.

Occasionally after his dinner, my father came into the kitchen to see if I had eaten my vegetables. If they were still on my plate, he would say, "Sit there until you eat them."

I hate the dry, disgusting peas and lima beans–they get stuck in my throat. They make me gag. The taste of the peas is disgusting. I hate sitting here for extra time, looking at those vegetables.

One day my mother noticed something in the kitchen, and said, "Angel, there's a strange smell in here. Is there something you didn't clean?"

"I don't think so, ma'am."

They looked everywhere. Two days later, "There's something rotten in this kitchen. We've got to find it." They looked everywhere again. My father joined the search.

He exclaimed, "It's coming from over here by this high chair. "&%$*$#, look at that." He chuckled at my creativity.

In my sister's former white metal high chair where I ate, the back curved around to each front edge. This created a kind of decorative tube on either side of the chair. I had dropped those nasty peas and lima beans down the tubes when Angel wasn't looking. I heard they had difficulty digging the rotten vegetables out of those tubes. I think, now, "Good for me!" I still don't like peas and beans.

My father continued to try to force me to eat those vegetables. I felt furious, which made eating anything almost impossible. I didn't know his intention—maybe he was concerned about my nutrition. I knew each bite he forced me to eat fed his passion for control.

Presently, when I eat dinner, I still leave a bit of something on my plate. My stubborn streak still operates.

My mother insisted I go to bed earlier than my sister because I was younger and needed more sleep. That may have been true, but I felt she was too eager to get rid of me.

Nighttime is the loneliest time. Sometimes I can hear my parents and sister talk and laugh while I'm lying in bed. There isn't much laughter in this house. If it happens, I want to be there. While I lie here, I worry about what my father will do if he comes into my room later. My body is so restless. I learn to rock myself to sleep.

I could relate to Angel's status. I felt like an underdog, myself. My parents made sure she "knew her place." Like me, she wasn't allowed to have an opinion.

In my mind, Angel is a member of the family and the best one. She's the only one who seems to notice I'm here. It's what she doesn't do as much as what she does do. Angel isn't mad or impatient with me. She's kind and gentle. She smiles at me.

My parents let Angel stay in our attic when she needed a place to live. This attic real estate featured extremes of heat in summer and cold in winter. There was no bathroom or toilet up there. I know she didn't use ours. Your guess is as good as mine regarding what she did.

Angel lived up there for about a year. She was required to be in the hot/cold attic when she wasn't doing some kind of work for us. I wasn't allowed to go up there to see her. Everything about Angel's life was a big secret, or—for my parents—it wasn't worth talking about. I don't know which.

My mother acquired a bell for summoning Angel to bring food, clear the table, etc. I can still picture my mother swinging that thing back and forth. Ding, ding, ding.

My sister, who rarely objected to anything, claimed: "This is seriously unkind."

My mother insisted, "Ringing that bell is more genteel than yelling for Angel. I will continue to use it."

I think ringing the bell made her feel powerful and classy. My mother came from farmers and was moving up the success ladder.

One September morning, when I was six, I got out of bed and asked, like I usually did, "Where's Angel?"

My mother replied lightly, "She's not here. She no longer works for us."

I was shocked. I couldn't breathe. "What do you mean?"

She replied, "Your father and I decided we don't need her anymore."

I groaned, "Oh, no. I want Angel to come back. I need her!"

My mother stated, firmly, "That doesn't matter. She's gone for good. She was a big expense. You girls are old enough now to help me more."

I couldn't believe it. I was screaming inside, "No, no, no."

That evening I was determined. I stood up straight and pushed my slouching shoulders back. I said to my mother and father, "I'm going to go find Angel. I want to live with her."

My father said, with a pained expression and a voice full of disgust, "No, you can't. You will get lost, and then you won't have anyone to take care of you. She's nobody. She's just some poor old black woman. We're your parents. We are the ones who matter."

My mother, while pinching her eyebrows together, shook her head and said, in her voice dripping with venom, "You don't know what's good for you. You don't deserve what you have. You'll be sorry someday."

My father said something cruel about "nigger toes," a coarse old slang term for the Brazil nuts he was eating, but also a mean swipe at Angel. He laughed. He had a way of trying to lighten things up that made me feel terrible.

I hate it when he talks about Angel or her people this way. I couldn't possibly feel worse than I do now. Will I never see her again? I can't believe this. My heart is dying. They don't know how I feel. They don't care how I feel. Angel is all I have. Angel is my mother, and I want to be with her.

When my real mother and I rode the streetcar downtown, I scanned the crowds trying to catch a glimpse of Angel. I looked for black faces, but none of them were her's.

Now I'm even more jealous of my sister because she has a mother and I don't.

The pain of this loss was enormous. I buried the memories of Angel as much as I could so I could go on living.

Months later, I heard my mother make a comment to her friend that made me sick. She said, "(my sister's name) really missed Angel after she left." Maybe my sister missed her, but I was hopelessly lost and going around in circles without her. My mother didn't notice. Or, did she say that in my presence to be mean?

After I was grown up, this grief was hidden, but not entirely. One clue was the way my eyes would tear up when I read P.D. Eastman's book, *Are You My Mother?*[1] to my children. This book is about a baby bird's distress when he discovers his mother has left the nest. He travels around to various objects and animals, pleading, "Are you my mother?" They all say no. Finally, the mother returns. Mother and child are reunited. Sigh.

I loved that book. I related to that story. While it hurt me to read it, the story connected me to myself. If I shed a tear, I would try to explain to my children without telling them much.

Another clue to my hidden grief was the pattern of my depressions. At midlife, I realized I had been depressed every fall for many, many years.

I dread that time. I hate it when the leaves fall. I hate even more when the crickets start to sing at the end of summer.

That's when that darkness grabbed me and sucked me in. Leaves falling and crickets singing—those were my body's clues to relive that devastating childhood loss.

Sometimes, in autumn, as an adult, I projected intense anger onto the people around me. Over the years, I broke up with boyfriends and other friends in the fall. I forced my first husband when I knew he was leaving for good, to move out at a moment's notice that fall. Problems seemed catastrophic at that time of year. I could hardly function.

These depressions worsened as I got older. In therapy, I tried, unsuccessfully, to attribute them to various problematic past events, including the death of my mother. Nothing clicked.

The last and best clue to my depressions was an old kitchen floor. My first husband and I had bought a historic house. I treasured the house. I was strangely and immediately drawn to the kitchen's old red-patterned linoleum. Every time I looked at it, something went off in my brain. One day while I was in the kitchen, I decided to sit down on the floor and try to figure out what was happening to me when I saw it.

The closer I get to the floor, the stronger I feel a sense of something old and familiar, along with warm, tender feelings. I notice I have other familiar, pleasant sensations in my body. I love just sitting here. It feels so good.

I considered this reaction while we settled in. Something reshuffled in my brain.

The color and pattern of this linoleum light up my memory. Could that be the same flooring I saw so many years ago when I played on the kitchen floor near Angel? It must be. It is!

Some memories come back. I re-experience the comfort and contentment I felt when I was with Angel. Her kind, quiet manner, and her soft voice make me feel warm and safe. She says sweet loving words while she gently helps me put on my clothes in the morning or washes dishes in the kitchen while I play.

I wish I could remember her words. They are lost. I stubbornly refuse to make them up. It was something like what Aibee says in the film, *The Help*:[2] *"You is kind, you is smart, you is important. That's so good."*

Over several years I discovered layers of profound grief—some while writing this book. There seemed to be no end to it. I finally released those painful feelings with energy healing and some inner child work. I lit candles to honor that child part of me who carried the grief. She was so sad. Then I could let her grow up, and I could let go of the pain. Finally, my body, mind, and spirit are mostly free of that sorrow.

Have you ever noticed how beautiful the leaves are in the fall in the Midwest? I just did.

Now I can acknowledge the gift of Angel's love. I had thought no one loved me when I was little. I am so happy to remember Angel did. I loved her too. I love her now. My therapist-self wants to rewrite the end of this story with Angel. What I needed most from my parents were an advance warning, a discussion, and some goodbyes with tears. First, I needed a conversation like the following:

Parent: "You really feel bad about Angel leaving."
Me: "Yes, I want her to come back right now."
Parent: "You must really like Angel a lot to feel so strongly about her leaving."
Me: "Yes, I do. I love Angel."
Parent (choking back personal feelings): "Oh, you love her? I didn't realize she was so important. I see she really is. You seem sad. I'm sorry this hurts you so much."
Parent listens and responds compassionately to what comes next, then continues: "We don't need Angel like we did when you were little, and we don't want to spend money to hire her, anymore. How can we help you with this? What would you like us to do?"
Me: "Keep her for five years."
Parent has Angel come back for a month (a week, a day) or at least to say goodbye. Soothes the grieving child. Tries to fill in the gap some, but doesn't hover, or tell her not to cry or feel the way she feels.

Rewriting this scenario and giving myself what I needed made me feel better— almost as if it had happened this way.

REFLECTIONS: A Broader View of My Parents

In this book, you might have noticed, I didn't call my parents Mother and Father. I called them my mother and my father. They gave me life, but very little parenting. My sister and I called them Mommy and Daddy even when we were grown. This sounded childish to me as a teenager. I tried to call my father "Dad" to announce and assert my teenage status. He mocked me. I gave that up. I didn't call him anything after that.

I've become a person who likes to see the big picture. I learned that from therapists. I want to see all the available new TV's, so I know I'm buying the best one for me. I look at all the possible consequences before I take action. I might sound overly cautious, but I call it thoughtful. It's much better than the plunge in/worry later approach I previously used.

I try to see cause and effect. Now I look for and leave room for alternative explanations. The other day I suddenly could see a bigger picture of my parents. At the same time, I could see my view of them had been stuck all this time.

What have I been missing in my representation of them? There was more to my parents than their relationship with me. Their intention was not to make me miserable. They were trying to survive in the world and find their way through their own traumatic childhoods. They were influenced by the same kinds of poor parenting they dished out. They were overly attached to what they wanted and what they thought was best for them. That may indicate a lack of appropriate concern by their parents for them. I do not know what kinds of horrors they experienced in their lives before or after I was born.

"Children should be seen and not heard" was a favorite saying when I was a child. Even good parents were more self-centered at the time I was born. I took my parents much too seriously. I accepted the identity they assigned to me. I needed to do that then; I do not need to do that now. I feel my attitude and my feelings toward my parents softening and shifting right now. In my mind, I see my parents becoming smaller and drifting further and further away behind me.

The world around me looks different now. The sun coming in the windows is sunnier and brighter. Colors are more colorful and pleasing. I see how the gourd-colored wall paint in this room makes the old wood floor glow. I feel the edges of my body and how they contain my insides. They aren't spilling out or mixed with my parents' innards. This means my boundaries are stronger. I am more complete in myself. I feel relieved and relaxed.

CHAPTER 4

Wounded and Coping Poorly

While writing the previous chapter, I was pleased to recognize that as a child, I was able to feel connected to Angel, and I was more tuned in to myself when I was with her. All those years later, when the happy memories surfaced (Chapter 3), I could recall more of what I saw, heard, and felt than at any other time in my childhood. Her love made that difference. Besides, I think she saved my life. At least, she saved my sanity.

I loved Angel. I counted on her. I felt she was the only person in the world who cared about me. Then she went on record in my heart as disappearing without saying goodbye. I was crushed. Looking back, I'm sure it was my parents' idea to dodge an emotional goodbye scene. My sister and I might cry or protest their decision.

After Angel left, I was suddenly a part of my family, yet I felt more unwanted than ever. Unconsciously, I decided to cut people out of my life. They would abuse, reject, or leave me.

If I needed anything, I would take care of it myself. I would be lonely, but the only time I felt safe was when I was alone.

A girl my age lived at the end of our street. Her father drove her to school every day. If they saw me walking to school, he'd stop the car and ask if I'd like a ride. I'd accept it, but I worried that I wasn't worth their trouble. They were kind to me.

The girl's father would say, "Any morning you would like a ride to school, just walk down to our house."

I'd reply, "Okay," but I never did it. I had separated myself from others. I had abandoned my real self and replaced it with a false self—what I thought my parents wanted. I was empty inside with little to say and much to hide.

Along with having nobody to prevent the incest, I had no one who could acknowledge it was happening or comfort me afterward. That created additional trauma.

Comforting didn't happen for me in my family. When I was little, if I fell and hurt myself, my mother would remark, "You never watch where you're going." She was correct. I wasn't really in my body or paying attention. She would leave me there on the ground. My sister would slip away. My father, if he were available, would clean and bandage the wound.

I think I was born smart. It didn't show. The stress of childhood sexual abuse and emotional neglect scrambled my brain. I needed to focus almost entirely on my safety and survival. To cope, I dissociated. That showed up as forgetfulness.

When I dissociated, I was uncomfortably detached from myself and my surroundings. My brain was foggier than usual. I felt as if I were nowhere. To forget my father had molested me the previous night, I blocked out everything else that happened at that time.

I forgot past experiences, people, places, and large blocks of time. I continued to do that long after the abuse ended. My children would say, "Remember our family vacation when we went to _____, and _____ happened?"

"No," I would respond. "Tell me about it."

Sometimes I pretended to remember. My children were distressed that I forgot those special times together. It hurt me, too. I couldn't explain it to them or myself. Fortunately, we have some good family memories and pictures.

I have always mixed up dates and times. When my children were little, I embarrassed them by taking them to their friends' birthday parties on the wrong day or hour. Later on, I didn't mind when they teased me. I hoped that meant my forgetting didn't hurt my children and they saw it was just another of my quirks. They tell me they always knew I loved them.

Both as a child and as an adult, I found ways to block out abuse memories. I would decide to eat the leftover pizza, for example. Before I arrived at the refrigerator, I would lose track of where I was going. Or, my hand would be on the refrigerator door handle, but I couldn't remember why I was there. I might start to do something else, like throw away some old food I found on a shelf. I'd probably follow through with the pizza eventually. This kind of experience is typical for older people, but it was something I did all my life.

I experienced a similar type of forgetting, which was also a form of dissociation when I had no task planned. Out of the blue, my mind would freeze and remain blank for about six seconds. Looking back, I believe the purpose of this behavior was to check my memory to see if any sexual abuse had recently happened.

I believe this forgetting developed in childhood when I especially needed to erase those times when my body would appear to betray me by reacting sexually to my father's abuse. Otherwise, my personal monster of panic and disgust for myself would eat me alive. Then I felt like an accomplice or even the instigator, as my mother claimed I was. This going blank also continued after the abuse ended.

Besides checking on the inside of me, I checked around the outside of me to determine if I was physically safe. I would frequently, and unconsciously, stop what I was thinking or doing to feel my body and the space around me. Nobody could see this. I didn't know I did it. This made some activities challenging. For example, as a young adult in college, I tried hard for years to learn to play the piano. I enjoyed it, but it was frustrating. I practiced three or four times as much as the other students in my piano class, yet I didn't improve like they did.

This is what was happening inside: When I automatically checked on my body, I lost track of my place in the music or where my fingers were on the piano keys. I couldn't avoid making mistakes. Neither the teachers nor I knew I regularly interrupted the focus of my attention. I just now figured that out.

The teachers and the music department had little sympathy. They assumed I didn't practice, in spite of my telling them I did. I couldn't complete the piano requirement for my music major. I dropped out of college when I was almost ready to graduate. I felt I had failed. However, I was glad to quit the madness of years of trying to do the impossible.

Reading books was uncomfortable for the same reason as the piano-playing, but at least when I read, I could go back and catch what I missed. To manage high school and college, I needed to read assignments several times because I didn't pay good attention.

I learned early in school that I could tune in to teachers, now and then, to determine if what they were saying was important. If it was, I took notes and studied them later. Then, the rest of the class time, I would be in outer space with a blank mind. This worked. My grades were above average. The exceptions were the piano classes and that wicked high school geometry which I will never understand.

In childhood, I was on pins and needles about whether I had done something right or wrong. My parents expected me to fail. I gained their attention by making mistakes. For that, I endured their caustic criticism, my father's teasing, and my feelings of failure.

I believe the advantage to the family of having me in the scapegoat role was that everyone else could feel better. I could be considered the cause of their unwanted feelings; I could be an excuse for their bad behavior. My mother could dump her unwanted emotions onto me. My father could feel in control and be one up.

Screwing up, not being on time, not getting things done, was a way of coping. That's how I got attention, but it cost me good feelings about myself and lowered my self-esteem even further.

When I worried about the future and the past, I avoided awareness of my present fear and loneliness. When I tried to be present, I had difficulty focusing and concentrating. My mother said I was absent-minded and "in a fog." Many years later a coworker at my first job would tell me I was "oblivious." They were right. I could see it in myself, but I couldn't fix it.

During my childhood and beyond, I felt lost, and I lost my belongings. Between school and home, for example, I would lose my sweater, books, or other school items. I realized I held onto objects very tightly. I would tell myself to lighten that death grip. I was acting out my grief from the loss of Angel by losing things repeatedly and holding tightly to what was still mine.

INSIDE INCEST was written for survivors of sexual and other abuse and those who live and work with them. The book is appealing to other people, as well. Its conversational style makes it easy to read and relate. It's engaging and informative and not technical. Common issues of family dysfunction, family secrets, alcoholism, codependency, and denial are involved, as well as survivor experiences such as dissociation.

The memoir part of this book is affirming to sex abuse and emotional neglect survivors. "Someone had similar experiences and pain. I'm not alone or crazy." This book shares the shame, and eventually, the gratitude which comes with the ability to cope and heal. This is a hero's journey, as well.

People who experience incest in childhood are vulnerable to being mistreated sexually and in other ways throughout their lives. They can lose their ability to establish boundaries and take care of themselves in challenging situations. This can result in rape and "Me Too" experiences.

Finally, this book is relevant to everyone because this devastation needs to be stopped, and that can't happen until people understand and speak freely about incest.

Growing up, I was shut down emotionally, except for periods of panic or anger about the abuse or being left out. I had no interests or hobbies, and I didn't play much. Sometimes, I could feel where my father had last violated me. So that some of my body parts wouldn't touch other body parts and remind me of what he did, I developed a kind of stiff-legged walk.

To survive in this family, I needed to give up my version of the truth and ignore my senses, my judgment, and my experience. I was squashed and suffocated. I felt excruciatingly lonely, worthless and always afraid.

Besides killing me with his abuse, I thought my father could kill me with his anger, even though he wasn't physically violent. I had to bottle up my own anger. Shutting it down caused my whole self to be shut down. I was so depressed, I didn't notice all my anxiety. I bit my fingernails and cuticles.

This is what I thought and felt: I don't want to do anything, be with anyone, or go anywhere. I don't need to learn anything. Someone else decides everything for me. I just go along with it.

A significant exception to all this lethargy occurred when I was eleven years old. One night as I was in bed trying to sleep, my father's classical music thundered from downstairs. I called down there, "That music is so loud, it's keeping me awake."

My father replied, "*^%$#^&%!"

I said, "I can't sleep, and I have school tomorrow."

My father growled, "This is my house. I can do what I want. "%^*&E^&! You only think of yourself. What you want is not important."

Rage boiled up from deep inside like it never has before or since. I threw on some clothes, ran out the door and took off running down the street.

I can hear the reader saying, "Oh, that poor little rich girl. The music was too loud, and she had to run away in her safe neighborhood for three hours. Big deal. Much, much worse things happen to me."

I reply, "I'm sure they do." That situation was a trigger for me. I put up with the horrible things my father insisted I do, but if I asked for simple consideration, it was too much for him. He could refuse. I couldn't. That's what made me angry."

To continue my story—in the warm spring darkness, I ran as fast as I could. The breeze I made from running cooled my burning face. Nature was with me. I felt more alive and powerful than I have ever felt before or since. It was amazing and exhilarating. This was outright rebellion, and I didn't care.

I ran until I came to the alley in back of the stores on a major cross street. (We had moved from the location I described in Chapter 1.) I dragged a large piece of cardboard to the back of a building so I could sit on the ground and lean against the wall. It was about 11:00 P.M. This was a safe neighborhood, but you never know that for sure at night in an alley.

It's so dark back here. I can hardly see anything. I've been here before. I know what this looks like in daylight. I'm still panting. I love this fantastic energy. Could I get this back when I return to my usual, dull self? What should I do now?

Oh! I see a bright light. Someone is driving through the alley and slowly passing a searchlight along the backs of the buildings. I'm so scared, I couldn't move if I wanted to. When the light reaches me, it shines above my head and barely misses me. Who is that? Did they call the police? I watch the car move slowly past me and leave the alley. Whew! I have no place else to go. It's obvious what I will do.

The door is locked. My mother answers the doorbell. I'm relieved. I don't see my father, but I'm nervous about what he's thinking and what he will do.

I asked my mother, "Can I come home now?"

She said, "Of course you can."

With a tremble inside, I said, "Is he still mad at me?"

My mother replied, "I don't want to talk about it now. I'm tired, and I'm going to bed."

Thanks a lot, Mom.

She never did talk about it. The man who can do whatever he wants was nowhere in sight.

The next day my father didn't look at me or speak to me. He continued to ignore me completely, day after day. I felt more shunned than ever before. I felt ashamed, too, but I told myself what I had done was okay. Myself didn't believe me.

After two long two weeks, my father returned to his normal behavior. He didn't say one word about what I'd done or what he'd done. No one in the family mentioned my running away. My adventure didn't seem real anymore. I thought I would be pushing my luck and could cause more grief if I brought it up. I wanted to tell someone how neat it was to feel so full of energy and life. I never did. Instead, I followed the rules.

Why didn't they blame me when it would have been justified? I suspect my father didn't want to admit he was wrong. You could say his silent treatment worked for him. I never ran away again. As for me, I am finally telling someone how great that rage-powered energy felt.

You may wonder why I'm not angry more often. Well, I've been there and done that, plenty. My anger is old and mostly spent, except when I discover something new. I've been with this stuff for a long time. I accept it, usually.

At the beginning of treatment, anger was my constant companion. I was furious when I realized the following, for example: As a child, vision problems reflected my inner state. The glasses I wore by age four didn't help much. I didn't want to see. My eyes didn't focus or work together as they are designed to do. My left eye wandered off toward the left. Did I watch for my father to come close or try to avoid seeing him when he was close? Sometimes I couldn't see what was directly in front of me. That makes sense, too. I didn't want to see what was directly in front of me.

As an adult, I discovered I had little depth perception until I worked on my childhood trauma in therapy. My depth perception came back in stages when I talked about, and could then "see," my childhood trauma. I could recognize the improvement when I looked toward the far end of a shopping mall. The view was no longer flat. It improved until eventually, it was 3-D. What a difference!

Now, when I see small children wearing glasses, I wonder why. I'm sure there are other causes of childhood vision problems besides sexual abuse. I want the prescribers of tiny glasses to ask if there is something in the child's life that the child might not want to see. They could report to Children Services if they were suspicious of abuse.

When I was about six years old, the girls in our neighborhood were all my sister's age—about three years older than I. My mother said my sister didn't need to include me in their play if she didn't want to. She didn't. I didn't want to be with them, but I felt hurt. I was left out again—by my sister. She continued to want nothing to do with me. I didn't know why. I assumed she thought I was unworthy of her company. Later on, when I did hang out with some girls or women, I made little effort to be a friend. I wanted them to choose me first so I could be sure they liked me before I would take a risk.

I was afraid to explore after-school activities. I wanted to avoid going home to those closed doors with nobody glad to see me. Around age eight, my parents let me stop at the local "dime store" on the way home. At every visit, I would stroll up and down each aisle and scrutinize everything. I killed as much time there as I could. I didn't talk to anyone or buy anything except gum.

One time I stole a small rubber ball. Nobody saw that. Afterward, I felt overwhelming guilt and self-hatred. It was as if I had emptied out a jewelry store. I didn't need any more of those feelings. I didn't steal again.

As a child, I had no one to help me. I wanted God to rescue me, or at least make me feel better. He didn't do either, as far as I could tell. My parents sent my sister and me to Sunday school. We alternated between the two churches next door. My parents didn't attend. They said they didn't believe in God. I figured if God did exist, he wouldn't want to help me, either.

Perhaps it's because of God that my coping included the desire to stay alive. Although I was miserable, I never contemplated suicide or hurting myself for more than a moment. Even so, I was alive, but I wasn't really living. Deep down, I felt I didn't deserve to live. Nobody wanted me.

As I write this, *I* want me. Right now, I feel blessed to be alive. The clarity I'm gaining about my life is precious. I'm grateful for it.

A unique memory puzzles me. When I was six, my father's sexual abuse increased in frequency and intensity. Following a particularly frightening abuse experience in his office, I went to my bedroom.

The walls of my room were painted blue; the wood trim and bed were white. The bed was covered with a hand-sewn quilt that was made, I think, by my mother's mother. It was daylight. I laid on my back on the bed and looked at the ceiling. I was still dissociating. I saw fascinating shapes form on the ceiling. I could make them come and go. I could change their color and size. I did that for a while. Then I said to myself—or I heard a voice from somewhere else command— "Don't do this anymore. You must stop now."

I understood that if I didn't cease making those pictures, immediately, I would go to a place of no return. I never tried that again. Looking back, I think that I was stopped (or I stopped myself) from hallucinating and becoming schizophrenic, or perhaps only psychotic. I would be trapped in a different reality.

Even though I shut out of my awareness much of the sexual abuse, my body remembered certain disgusting childhood abuse events with my father. This manifested, for example, in my clenched jaws and when I choked, gagged, and coughed throughout my life, or when I threw up from drinking too much alcohol in my late teens as I tried to deal with my not-so-hidden emotional pain. Years later, my jaws spontaneously released their tension for the first time. I had just finished a session with a therapist. As I stood in a grocery store checkout line, I felt a dramatic jaw relaxation. I tried to act as if nothing was happening just as I did during the abuse.

My irritable father had forced me to do this terrifying thing at two years old. I was supposed to like it and please him. I resisted. That pocket of trauma became isolated from the rest of me, except that I remembered the nasty things he said that day.

All through my childhood and adolescence, anyone's brief mention of sex triggered massive amounts of shame and disgust. At age ten, in Girl Scout camp the first night, we were in our beds in one big room. Some girls started to talk about sex—how to do it.

That triggered me. My body tensed up. I panicked. At that moment, I had no conscious awareness of my secret sex life. I had brought the other part of me to camp. That other part didn't know about sex, and she didn't want to know. I was trapped.

Another girl said to the group, "I don't think we should talk about this."

Others replied, "What's the matter with you? Are you a baby? Too bad. We're going to talk about it anyway."

And they did. I isolated myself from the group as much as I could, and anxiously waited to go home. I said nothing to anybody, as usual.

This next event I describe was much different from my other memories, but the outcome was similar. Somehow, this time, my ironclad self-protection failed me. I don't know how that happened. I was sixteen years old—maybe that's how.

It was New Year's Eve. We were standing in the dark under clotheslines in his parents' musty-smelling basement laundry room. A few other couples were in there with us, but we ignored each other on purpose. More couples were talking in the room next door where we were all supposed to be.

Neither of us was a talker. We kissed, and we kissed. My knees felt so weak I was afraid I'd collapse onto the concrete floor. I was excited and not too scared. Periodically, my date's mother would yell down the basement stairs, "Turn that light back on!"

My date would duck his head under the clotheslines and dodge the hanging clothes to turn the light on. Then he quickly turned it off again. In retrospect, this seemed like a game he and his mother were playing, and one they had played before.

It was rare that I went to a party. Usually, I would have little to say and be anxious to leave, but this time I was disappointed when the party ended. Afterward, I dwelled on this experience for days while in a lovely romantic trance. I didn't have anyone else to tell, so I retold this story to myself.

Then, my thinking started to change. I saw myself spoil this sweet memory. What was innocent and natural gradually turned contemptible. What was the matter with me? How could I lose myself this way? It looks, now, like I became my mother. What a disappointment when fear and shame took over. I avoided that boy in school. I focused on his acne when I saw him, so I wouldn't like him. I never spoke to him again.

He probably thought it was his acne that scared me away. It was his tenderness.

In a high school science class, I was assigned to sit at a two-person table with a popular boy who seemed friendly. During the dull times, we wrote notes back and forth. That was highly unusual for me, and fun. I noticed his writing became a little suggestive at times, but I felt safe enough.

During a science class demonstration, we all stood in front of the teacher to watch. For some reason, we were outside, because the picture in my mind has me standing on green grass. The sun was shining. The teacher told us to move closer so we could see his experiment.

This boy crowded in behind me. I felt something hard poking at me in back. I froze to that spot of ground. He didn't move. I didn't say a word. I felt angry, betrayed, and ashamed. I never spoke to him again, either. I felt horrible for days. He had triggered my childhood trauma as well as creating a new one. I told no one.

Coping with my childhood was stressful and annoying. It didn't make sense. I tried to cover up and then hide the cover-up, as well. That was too much work. It made me feel stupid. I was sure other people didn't do what I did.

As I write this, I'm surprised and saddened at the far-reaching effects of my childhood mistreatment. I feel the pain and exhaustion of so many years of secretly trying to endure and manage my brokenness and shame. Now, looking back at that, I feel so much better. I understand the reasons for my behavior. I'm angry it was necessary to do all that, but I'm glad I didn't give up.

I wanted someone to love me. In spite of all my fears and unresolved trauma, I wanted to have a boyfriend in high school. Some boys were interested. I looked like I was playing "hard to get," which girls did then because I didn't talk much. But I wasn't playing hard to get—in my mind, I was playing with fire.

Flirting was out of the question because of that five-year-old trauma I described in Chapter 1. I knew I was missing something special that happens between two people who were attracted to each other, and I was envious when I saw couples flirting. It looked comfortable and fun when they did it, but it seemed way too dangerous for me.

I have memories of times when boys or men would ignore my keep-away signals and try to flirt with me. Somehow, I attributed their behavior to the clothing I was wearing. Without knowing the reason, or even that I did it, I completely stopped wearing whatever I had been wearing when that happened. I hoped to look good, but unconsciously, I didn't want to look *that* good.

The clothing I stopped wearing included the prettiest and best dress I ever sewed for myself after I had considerable practice in sewing. It was red and white checked fabric with blue trim which I had sewn on both the dress and shawl. The shawl was to cover bare shoulders if needed. I wore it one time. The following event occurred when I was married to my first husband.

At a concert, a man I knew who played in the orchestra, said, "You look really great in that dress. I haven't been attracted to my wife in a while. She hasn't been making an effort to look good. I don't know why."

I was speechless. I felt disgusted and contaminated instead of flattered. Afterward, I put the dress away. Years later— about twenty of them—I hung it on the wall of the room where I sewed. It still looked beautiful and just right for me. Of course, it no longer fit.

While writing about this dress, I noticed I was avoiding something I didn't want to feel. I decided to invite my sadness in, as an honorable guest, as suggested by the poet Rumi in his poem, "The Guest House." Once I faced it, I realized I felt hopeless about this lost opportunity and the many others in which I stopped myself from being myself and flourishing. At that moment, I realized I had something I liked in me that I wanted to free up and enjoy. I made a commitment to appreciate and honor what is unique and creative in myself when I see it. That part felt good. I did it, and I'm still doing it. It feels great!

In high school and beyond, I harbored conflicting feelings of repulsion and attraction to boys, dates, and sex. In the presence of males, I silently relived the fear and anxiety of my sexual abuse without knowing it. Actually, I was afraid of everyone, not just boys.

I felt sexually inadequate and ashamed of my body. I was nice-looking, but I wouldn't have liked my body no matter how I looked. I was terrified of the idea of intercourse. I was careful to avoid it, but I was blind to the risks I took to handle my massive discomfort about sex—I drank alcohol. Drinking a lot on dates jeopardized my safety but decreased my fear of boys. That made me vulnerable to being taken advantage of or attacked. Neither happened on dates, except for one time where no drinking took place.

I drank daily for years, along with my first husband, while I focused on my husband's drinking. Fortunately for me, I didn't become an alcoholic. Many people are not so lucky in that regard. When my emotional pain lessened with my healing, my desire to drink, and my consumption of alcohol diminished.

Alcohol numbed my pain. It's common for survivors to use something for that purpose. However, drinking, drug use, gambling, overeating, overworking, etc., slow down a person's healing because they cover up the pain. I have no doubt drinking was one reason my recovery took so long. I am responsible for that.

Avoidance of pain is the enemy of healing. I regret the time I lost, but I remember how severe the pain was. Treatment is available for substance abuse and childhood sexual abuse together. It helps manage that struggle between feeling the pain and killing the pain.

As a therapist, I want to say it's typical for women who were violated at a very young age to feel somewhere between scared and terrified of regular sexual activity when they reach the appropriate age. Nothing ruins the pleasure of adolescent or adult sex like early childhood incest.

For some survivors, the abuse has the opposite effect. They may seek sexual activity and have many sexual relationships, often with inappropriate partners. This may be due to sexual abuse beginning at a later age, or other factors. Each of these reactions comes with its own complications. I have focused on the first one since that was my experience.

In adulthood, I enjoyed the preliminaries of sex except for the shame I felt. I still dreaded intercourse. The first times two times I did that, I was with my husband-to-be. I experienced horrible flashbacks. I dissociated. I couldn't understand what was happening to me. How could sex be this terrible? I had not yet recalled that I'd been forced into that experience before with my father. What did Joe think about my reaction? He thought I would get over it.

I grew to like nonsexual touch. My experiences with sex became much better over time, but sometimes I was a disappointment to both of us. I had a "want to do it/don't want to do it" inner conflict. I couldn't make myself initiate sex.

Joe didn't complain much. Sometimes he found someone else. I hated that. I had seen signs that he might be inclined to cheat—he wasn't really willing to give up charming and attracting other women. It wasn't until much later, because I was so busy trying to cope with sex, that I recognized how big a problem my sexual issues were for him.

Having my first child with my unresolved sex abuse issues was disturbing and joyful at the same time. I was uncomfortable because of the medical attention to the place where the baby comes out, and joyful about the baby you get. The places where that baby was supposed to eat seemed more about sex than baby nourishment to me.

I loved my children, and I worried a lot as their parent. I wanted to do an excellent job as a mother, yet I felt utterly unprepared and lacking a role model. I couldn't share the depth of my feelings of inadequacy with anyone. No books had yet been written on raising children except the original one by Dr. Spock. It wasn't helpful for what I needed.

Joe called the shots, making the decisions in favor of himself and his career, and I let him. I was unhappy and depressed. I had expected to feel better being married. My fantasy was that Joe would take care of my needs and give me all the love I missed. He didn't. I couldn't decide what to do with myself and my life. With no career or job yet, my life was at an all-time low.

Joe loved to build model trains. His escape from reality looked attractive to me. I decided to learn to sew, so I could make window curtains to save money like my mother did.

My mother was an excellent seamstress. She sewed in the room you had to walk through to get to my bedroom in the house where I grew up. She made clothes for my sister and me. I objected to them because they were too different from the other kids' clothes and she didn't ask me what I wanted. My sister objected when she made the same outfit for both of us because then my sister was forced to look like me. My mother didn't teach me to sew.

She wouldn't admit she liked to sew, but I knew she did. My mother would stand outside in warm weather between our house and the two churches where my sister and I attended Sunday school. There she would accept compliments from other women about how well dressed her daughters were, and about her sewing prowess. I get that. I like it too when people appreciate what I create.

With minimal knowledge from my two Home Economics sewing classes in school, and trial and error attempts, I taught myself to sew. After the curtains, I learned to sew some of my own clothing. That made me feel I had accomplished something. It bumped up my low self-esteem a notch. Besides that, it was fun. It was something I looked forward to when the children napped and for many years after that.

About my social growth: I have explained what I was like on the inside. Now, I want to describe what I think other people saw from the outside. I was quiet, timid, standoffish, and easy to overlook. As an adult, in a group meeting or on an airplane, if there was an empty seat next to me, the latecomer chose the empty seat next to someone else. That happened a lot. Later on, I watched to see if this still occurred so I would know when I was no longer scaring people away.

Apparently, it was easy to see that my energy and vibrations were low. I had a dark cloud around my head. I didn't smile or laugh much. Once, an employer tried to take a picture of me for her advertising. She kept saying, "Let's try it again. Now, smile."

Neither of us could get me to smile and look like I meant it. I was mortified. At that time, I felt my true self was exposed, and I was inadequate as hell. I felt something was seriously wrong with me; I think this woman did, too. She smiled beautifully and often.

Besides smiling, two more significant life requirements were compromised by my childhood abuse. I had no sense of direction. I literally couldn't find my way around the block. I was easily lost. That problem improved when my kids gave me a GPS for Christmas (with love).

The other was my difficulty getting to sleep and staying asleep. By the age of 35, I had developed severe insomnia. Much of my father's sexual abuse had taken place after I was in bed and asleep. I couldn't shake the unconscious fear every night that I would be abused again. I had flashbacks of childhood terror. I feared I might die from the next abuse. No one would know or help me.

The tension from the anticipation of further abuse—even though on a conscious level, I knew it could no longer actually happen—spoiled my early evenings, too. I couldn't concentrate on anything. I didn't know why I felt so uncomfortable with myself, even as more and more years went by with no further abuse.

My experience of myself was unbearable at other times, too. I felt there was little of me left after my parents did what they did and what I continued to do to myself. I still blamed myself for everything. I admired and envied people who acted real, but for me, it wasn't safe to share anything personal, in case the wrong information came out. I wanted badly to be whole and to feel good. It felt agonizing to consider asking for help and letting someone into my private experience. I figured the work would be painful because when I thought about all this, I felt worse. Nevertheless, I started counseling soon after I was married the first time.

My new husband heard of a nearby mental hospital where Master's level psychology students practiced on the public in inexpensive outpatient services. I took the step, although I felt massive anxiety. I was scared that I would make a mistake and look foolish.

After saying hello, my psychology student gave me a Rorschach test. This was a collection of blurry-looking pictures that could be interpreted in various ways. What people thought they saw in the pictures was believed to reveal something about their emotional state. I avoided identifying those which looked like penises and sexually suggestive scenes. The following week she showed me several of those pictures again and asked me once more to describe what I saw. At the age of 23, I could not speak of penises and sexual intercourse. She pointed out my avoidance again.

I felt deeply, to my core, humiliated. I was ashamed just because the subject was sex. I felt blamed because I had done something terribly wrong that had to do with sex. And this woman wanted me to speak about the unspeakable.

I remember her one helpful sentence. "Something must have happened to you early in life." By that time, I didn't trust her. I went back for too many sessions and talked about nothing. Then she left the hospital.

Recently, for an assignment in a writing group, I wrote an essay on that first therapy experience. Finally, I knew what happened to my psychologist. She left that job to search for more missing penises.

Finding the humor in that situation helped free me from the humiliation I still experienced when those old feelings were stirred up. I think that beginner therapist meant well, but she used poor judgment. The Rorschach is a relic now.

Back at that clinic, they gave me a replacement psychology student. In our first session, I said, "I don't think my parents loved me." My male student therapist replied, "Of course they did."

Oh, so I'm wrong again.

He was too much like my parents. I didn't return.

After those two false starts, I was still befuddled about who I was and how I felt. I decided to solve my problem by myself. I volunteered to assist with the inpatient sewing activities at that psychiatric hospital. I did want to help, but my real motivation was to compare myself with the mental patients and determine if I was crazy.

What I saw was an appalling scene—I can still picture it—in a huge room with many patients who were whacked out on heavy drugs. Most were sprawled over the furniture and couldn't prop themselves up. I felt scared for them. I asked a nurse if they were okay. She said those patients were waiting for the initial effects of their drugs to wear off so they could go home. Those particular drugs had powerful side effects and are rarely used these days.

For obvious reasons, most patients were uninterested in sewing. I wished I could do something more helpful than my assigned task. For the first time, I was grateful I didn't belong to the group. I decided I was okay—I wasn't crazy. I appreciated my present circumstances. I was still confused about my life.

REFLECTIONS

At that time, I was vulnerable and unaware. I didn't know what I didn't know. Eventually, I would become determined to look inside and deal with what was there. That would be the key to my healing.

HEALTH FOOD FOR THOUGHT

It was so inappropriate and sad.

As I waited with my groceries in a shabby health food store loaded with good-for-you-food, an elderly woman sat down on the bench next to me. Her voice had a faraway quality as she told me—a complete stranger—about her childhood sexual abuse. She talked as much to herself as to me. I told her I was sorry that had happened to her. In less than five minutes, this precious, still grieving old woman gave me a gift of sharing.

It was a warning, too. I said to myself, "This could be me in fifty years."

CHAPTER 5

The Healing Begins

After those discouraging therapy attempts, I took a break. Then, I saw therapists off and on during the next few decades. Each of them taught me something valuable. At first, therapy was a risky experiment in trusting and sharing my inner self with a safe person. I accepted feedback and applied it when I could. One therapist succeeded in showing me the value of knowing my feelings and how to identify them. Before that, I only knew how to avoid feelings.

I was anxious during my appointments. I worried the therapist would judge me negatively. When I felt less self-conscious, I spent much of my session time complaining about my husband. I wanted him to be more attentive and available. I thought my problems would be solved if Joe would reduce his drinking and give me the consistent love and support I needed.

As time passed, Joe's drinking became a smokescreen. Focusing on him allowed me to avoid feeling the pain of my own problems. My therapist would say, "What about you? Why don't you work on yourself?" I thought I was working on myself. I didn't have much of a self; I had only a speck of self-awareness.

My marriage was everything to me. An Al-Anon joke describes codependency perfectly: you are drowning, and someone else's life passes before your eyes. Your focus is on the other person instead of yourself. That was me.

At Alanon meetings, I failed at learning to detach from the drinker—that is, to say and do nothing to keep the user from suffering the consequences of his behavior. However, I did succeed in learning to believe in a higher power. That gave me something to hold onto. I was going to need it.

Back then, Adult Children of Alcoholics group meetings educated attendees about the effects of growing up in an alcoholic, dysfunctional family. This information amazed me. The meetings made my head spin. They described my family of origin—family roles, family secrets, denial. I wasn't crazy after all. To some extent, it applied to my present family, too.

Another revelation was Inner Child work. That concept related to parts of me getting stuck at the age when the trauma occurred. I knew this concept fitted me. I knew I had parts. I learned that from a therapist.

I taught myself Assertiveness Training from books—how to stand up for myself, say no, ask for what I want, etc.—and I shared the information with my children, my husband, and eventually, my clients. That helped me feel powerful. These skills are invaluable for survivors.

I learned outstanding concepts from the therapist I admired. The first was how to do healing work. She told me, "Awareness is curative." If you become fully aware of what's going on with you regarding a particular issue, you can resolve it. That was a tool and a direction that changed my life. (I show you this tool in Chapter 9.) When you use it, you become more acquainted with your inner self. This is desirable and necessary for healing.

Here's an example: While folding laundry one day when I was married, with little children and no outside job, from deep in my gut came a blast of anger. I felt used and unappreciated. This family was taking advantage of me. I shouldn't have to be doing this laundry.

Then I said to myself, "Wait a minute. These feelings are out of proportion to this situation. They are too strong. My husband works and supports us. I take care of everything at home. That's the deal we have. Why do I feel so angry?" I didn't have a clue.

Now, I know. This was about my childhood. This frustration is a trigger, and triggers give you clues about what to work on. I misinterpreted the feelings as being about that current laundry because the only way feelings are experienced is in the present. Of course, it's a childhood memory. It's about my parents' treatment, and it's about chores, perhaps, but really, it's about sexual abuse and everything else that was forced on me as a child. That's why those feelings were so intense.

I disguised the anger from my unacknowledged trauma in other ways, too. I projected it on my first husband. I yelled at my children. I would wake up in the morning feeling so guilty, and promise myself I wouldn't do that today; then I would yell at them again. I was like my mother—though, I hope, not nearly as bad.

My favorite thing to do when my childhood trauma had me feeling furious was to smash old dishes I didn't need as hard as I could on the garage floor. The difficulty I had with that was having to clean up the mess afterward.

Healing trauma is about facing your feelings when they show up. We can find ways to deny or avoid feelings. We can shoo them away like flies in summer, but then they will come back just like the flies; or we can look at those feelings and tolerate them, sometimes with difficulty.

We can allow feelings to exist without judging ourselves for having them—even though we don't like them and want to get rid of them. The same is true for those uncomfortable body sensations from sexual abuse. You can visit them and then back away until you can tolerate them. I ask of a feeling or body sensation, "What are you telling me?" Sometimes it will get stronger. If you let the feeling stay, and allow yourself to feel it, it will hurt some more and then, possibly, go away for good. Or, you will have the opportunity to acknowledge it when it comes back the next time.

In one of our sessions, my favorite therapist told me, "You don't take up any space." To comprehend that, I needed to observe it in other people. We can see people who are "invisible" like I was, but we don't notice them much. Their bodies are pulled in and numbed out, with little of their energy emanating outward. I struggled with that issue for years until I was brave enough to want to be seen and heard.

This therapist was my first-ever role model. She demonstrated appropriate therapist boundaries, so I didn't know much about her, but I admired her warm, smart, genuine attitude. She didn't take any guff. She showed an air of confidence and comfort in her own skin that I wanted. I didn't want hers. I wanted my own.

"Therapists raised me," as one of my clients would tell me a few years later about herself. While in therapy, I learned how to set and maintain boundaries, plan ahead, look in advance for consequences, see the big picture, and many other life skills.

When I faced the frightening possibility that my shaky marriage might not survive, I decided to return to college. I wanted to become a therapist. My current job was not challenging. I wanted counseling to be my career, whether I was married or not. I had found I could relate well to people with problems. I hoped to understand my childhood.

I knew I had a lot of work to do on myself before I was prepared to be a professional. I was motivated. I did it with therapy, additional therapist training, and my college program.

Finally, after a few years, I was ready to take the risk for myself and for whoever would be my clients. I was fascinated with the clients and the counseling experience, and I still am. I was honored that people in need would share the personal details of their life with me. We are all so different from each other. We are all so much alike.

By that time, I was a skilled listener, and I had good ideas. The client did most of the talking. It's inappropriate for therapists to share their abuse history. With survivors, I said only that I had some personal experience with abuse. Being helpful made me feel good. My clients knew I was sincere in my efforts. I liked communicating on a deeper level than social chit-chat allows. It was time and social exposure limited. I felt safe.

I was capable as a counselor but less relatable than I am now. My relationship with non-clients remained problematic. It was based on fear and history. I was aware I still had an inner conflict regarding my need for love and approval while I continued to maintain distance from others.

This came to the forefront when my husband and I took a trip to Europe, where I was meeting some of his extended family there for the first time. Joe's relatives spoke English and the women were delighted to see Americans. These relatives seemed more mentally healthy than his American family.

One day we visited an older family member. She brought out pictures and more pictures of everyone in this European branch of Joe's family. One by one, she described each person in detail—his or her personality traits, skills, and relationships. Her face glowed with pleasure as she spoke lovingly about her family. She explained, "This is Trudy. She's adorable. She has beautiful blonde hair. Her boyfriend's name is John. She plays the violin well and hopes to play in an orchestra when she finishes school."

That loving recognition and caring, which I hadn't heard for myself—or anybody else, for that matter—cracked open a mysterious, deep well of grief. I began to cry. I couldn't stop. I wept on and off throughout the rest of the trip and after I arrived back home. I felt intense sadness, confusion, and the worst embarrassment of my life. My attempts to explain just made me cry harder, so I gave that up and over-apologized instead. His relatives acted as if this were no big deal. The women exuded warmth and caring; I hadn't experienced that either. They weren't remotely related to me, but they treated me better than my original family ever had.

Having people close to you who know you and talk to you, express interest, and describe how special you are, makes a big difference in one's self-esteem. Now that I knew how needy I was, I decided to be more loving and accepting of myself. Grieving those past losses allowed me to dare to get closer to others. I'm grateful I never had another crying jag like that.

My husband remained unusually distant during that European trip. Before my crying spell, I had tried to enjoy this adventure with him, but I couldn't seem to connect. I found out later he was having an affair at home. It's a good thing I wasn't aware of it on this trip (although I knew it, unconsciously). That affair would require several months of additional crying and a lot of anger.

After our thirty years of marriage, my husband wanted a divorce from me and a permanent relationship with that other woman. Our separation plunged me into severe grief, while all my earlier losses exploded into my present life. It was a terrible time. I was depressed. I felt lost.

Between my appointments at work, I'd lie down on my client couch as often as I could. I had no energy. I tried but failed, to act like my usual self the rest of the time. I transferred my marriage cases to other therapists and toughed it out at work. I noticed my self-esteem sinking lower than low. I could barely hold myself together. I felt I was missing a vital body part like an arm or a leg—but not my heart, because I could *feel* that hurt. I was so miserable, I wanted to say to some of my clients, "You think you have trouble? That's nothing. Listen to this..."

When I was at home alone and overcome with anger, I hit an old metal window fan with a tennis racket. I whacked that fan as hard as I could for as long as I wanted. I felt more powerful and somewhat relieved after expending that energy and making all that noise. It would release some of the rage layered on top of all my other feelings, which seemed to help me out of my paralysis. Sometimes, after I hit the fan, I would cry when I had exposed the grief underneath the rage. It sounded like wailing. This felt painful but relieving. Fortunately, no one besides my cat could hear that racket with the racket.

My therapist told me, "Ninety percent of your grief is due to your childhood trauma, and only ten percent to your divorce."

I replied, "You are mistaken." Eventually, I discovered I was mistaken. Without knowing it, I was reliving the emotional nightmare of abandonment by my parents and Angel. My husband's departure was a repetition of these losses. Present losses usually stir up and expose the pain of unresolved past ones.

Divorce was the worst/best thing for me. I wouldn't have left Joe myself, because I "loved" him. I was too dependent and codependent to dare to be alone. I was terrified of being permanently alone. I give thanks to Alanon meetings for the support and the Serenity Prayer—I wore it out. I know that prayer helps many people. It's simple and powerful. Here it is, in case you need it:

"God, grant me the serenity to accept the things I cannot change, the courage to change the things I can, and the wisdom to know the difference."

Around the time of my separation and divorce, I finally acknowledged to myself the severity of my father's sexual abuse. This was all too much to tolerate at one time. Putting one foot ahead of the other was all I could do, barely.

I sought out individual and group therapy for sexual abuse survivors. The group was supportive of my divorce pain. One of the members befriended me and shared invaluable lessons on how to be single after a long marriage. This friend tolerated my sour mood when we went to the movies. I didn't know how she could stand me, but I was glad she did.

At first, when working on my sexual abuse issues, I argued fiercely with myself about whether it had actually happened. *I know it happened. It didn't happen. I remember it. Maybe I imagined it.*

I'd stop doubting myself for a while, but the dialogue would start again. This "I know it happened" issue was mixed in with my "terrible person" debate.

The abuse was my fault. I don't think it was my fault. My parents were right about me. They didn't know me. I'm a terrible person—that's why bad things happen to me.

Finally, I told myself to just accept the idea that I'm worth fixing, due to all the damage I could clearly see and feel.

Get on with it.

Therapy helped me understand and normalize my abuse experience. That means recognizing what you feel is reasonable for the experience you've had. Although it sounds absurd, having the argument above is typical.

I had never lived alone. I could feel what seemed like all the loneliness of my entire life when no one else was in the house. I would suffer from nausea and feelings of dread on my way home from work. My children were on their own by this time, but my daughter came back to stay temporarily. It broke my heart to lose both my husband and the home I loved but couldn't afford to keep. I found another house which was just right for me, and another husband, although he showed up fifteen years later.

That fifteen years would give me time to learn many excellent lessons and prepare myself for what would come next. But first, I hid out in my new place and licked my wounds. I examined my messed up life. I needed to learn to take care of myself and to recover from divorce and childhood trauma. I needed to figure out how to manage relationships with men if it wasn't too late.

Fixing up a different house distracted me from my pain. It helped me feel competent. I managed to do hard physical work. I loved the decorating part. One son helped me start a garden. In time, I enjoyed the first place which was all mine.

The house was my focus. My cute little cat was my partner. I chose her from the cat rescue place because she stuck her foot out of the cage and wanted to play. At home, she would greet me with meows. I could hear them as I pulled into the garage. She sat on my lap. She loved me.

The teacher in my yoga class didn't even like me. She wanted everyone to look happy doing their poses. I looked like crap. My body was inflexible. She wanted lots of love and praise, but I gave her only money. Even so, I stayed in her class for thirteen years. It was the only one near my house.

She was a fine yoga teacher, except for her neediness. I could understand that.

One time she shared with the group that her son had been molested by an older woman. She said they both thought it was a great learning opportunity. I suggested that the experience can damage a boy, as well as a girl. That didn't increase my popularity with her, but I wished he could know that if he needed to know it.

During my separation and divorce, my physical condition deteriorated. I had been healthy and health-conscious. Now, I was allergic to almost all food. My energy was poor. My thick hair was falling out at an alarming rate. I was a physical, emotional, and spiritual wreck. I used alternative doctors and methods to eliminate rather than cover up the source of my symptoms.

In my work, I came across the Adverse Childhood Experience (ACE) questionnaire. It validated my suspicion that my physical and emotional problems were likely due to childhood trauma and grief. The effects of unresolved trauma often worsen with age. (See the ACE questionnaire in Chapter 9).

Attachment theory, which is popular now, described the effects of different styles of parental behavior on early childhood trauma. It didn't look like my childhood problems were all my fault.

Books and videos on relationship difficulties helped me discover what went wrong in my marriage and what to do differently in case I had another chance at love. Eventually, dating was challenging and felt good. Sex with a few carefully screened men was enjoyable after years with one partner and then nothing.

The one man I really cared about in my internet dating effort seemed entirely unlike my father and my ex-husband. He was different in looks, behavior, sense of humor, and other characteristics. He shared two similarities: he drank a lot, and he had another girlfriend in a nearby city. Of course, I had to discover those behaviors myself. This brought on severe pain from earlier losses when I experienced the confusion and figured out what he was hiding.

How could I do that to myself again? I was heartbroken once more. I ended the relationship. I was finished picking those men. I realized the right man for me would not feel familiar and comfortable like the men who usually attracted me. I needed a new set of criteria for choosing—another lesson learned but not yet tested. A little therapy helped me solidify my learning.

Here are the excellent lessons I learned from my divorce and dating:

- I learned to be independent, self-sufficient, and resourceful—because I could, and because that was what I wanted, after I decided it was preferable to helplessness. I survived. First, I floated and then I swam to safety. Later, I began to enjoy the trip.

- It was my job and my joy to discover who I was and what made me happy. I needed to create happiness for myself. Others can only contribute to it. Therapists and my experience showed me that my expectations of men who don't have much to give were inappropriate and unattainable.
- I could love the parts of me that I, and others, had ignored as a child. I needed to be around people who treated me well. I needed to do the same for them.
- I learned I couldn't fix someone else during my therapy, no matter how hard I tried. I could make critical decisions for myself about that relationship or change what I did and who I was in the relationship. I could only change myself.
- I learned to direct my attention toward men who treat women with respect, and when in a relationship with a woman, provide consistent love and support (although none will be perfect).
- Facing my divorce trauma and my childhood trauma would make my other goals achievable and give me some freedom from the past.

I was pleased with my progress. But…

I still don't understand. I feel so much shame in my daily life. I feel so much shame from the past. Was the abuse my fault? Who was right? What was real? I need answers. It's not enough just to

survive after what I've been through. Life must be worth living. I
will do whatever is necessary to make that happen.

Certain practices helped me to achieve my goal to feel
better. They were free and priceless. I started the first one
after I noticed how often I spoke to myself as harshly as
my parents had. I decided to replace my parents' critical
voices in my head with my kind words. For example, "you're
so stupid," turned into, "I need to do that differently next
time." To develop a more loving attitude toward myself, I
put positive affirmations on my desktop for daytime use.
I loaded some encouraging, enlightening voices of others
onto my iPod and listened to those at night in bed, especially
when I couldn't sleep.

Then I practiced being in the present moment. Reading
Eckhart Tolle's book, *The Power of Now*,[3] I was astounded
how he could remain present. Staying in the moment for
more than a moment was difficult for me. I felt more alive
when I experienced being in the present. I was more tuned
into other people and myself. I paid better attention. When
I became aware that I was back in the past or in the future,
I could send my mind to the present for a while.

The third practice was "inner child" work. As an adult, I
was playing that role but often didn't feel like an adult. My
wounded parts needed to be acknowledged, nurtured, and
nudged to grow up. I talked to them and gave them what
I had missed as a child—love, reassurance, understanding,
compassion. I validated their feelings. It's never too late. If

I did that when I wasn't feeling good, all of me would feel better. I had three inner children who I treated as one since I didn't have a multiple personality disorder.

I continued to struggle with physical complications. I could feel much of the sexual trauma was still lodged in my body. As a therapist, I was familiar with different healing methods. I had trained in a version of EMDR—Eye Movement Desensitization—and taught myself to do EFT—Emotional Freedom Technique—which is also known as "tapping." (These are explained in Chapter 9.) Both of these methods were effective. I used them with clients, too.

While viewing health and spiritual development videos on the internet, I encountered the energy healing work of Dr. Bradley Nelson. He is a chiropractor and the author of The Emotion Code and Body Code system (www.drbradleynelson. com; www.healerslibrary.com).[4]

The concept was familiar to me; I had seen other energy healing videos and had experienced Reiki treatments. Years ago, I had worked with Louise Hay's early book, *You Can Heal Your Body*.[5] Her book explained how emotional problems are expressed in the physical body. Dr. Nelson has developed a complete energy healing system. In his video, Dr. Nelson stated that some of the emotions which occur during traumatic events, instead of being released, can become trapped in the body. Later, they may create energy imbalances in the body.

An energy imbalance can cause physical, emotional, or spiritual problems in a person's life. These imbalances may manifest as physical pain, depression, anxiety, disconnection from others, lack of fulfillment, and more. Dr. Nelson showed how these negative energies can be released to restore balance to the body. You can buy this program and learn to do it yourself, or you can hire a practitioner—or both. (See Chapter 9 and Dr. Nelson's website.)

I knew I had trapped emotions galore. Although following my gut instincts was unusual for me then, I dove into learning the Emotion Code. It covers emotional, mental and spiritual issues, while the Body Code covers everything physical and includes The Emotion Code.

The people I told about my plan were skeptical of the method and questioned my need to work on myself. They said, "Why would you want to learn an entirely new kind of treatment? Forget about the past. You've done enough work on yourself, already. Life is short. Move on."

My response was, "I want to feel better. In fact, I want to feel great, and I believe I will." Those skeptics let me do Emotion Code work on them so I could become certified and then learn the Body Code, too. They were impressed with how well this method works. In time, my energy healing clients would experience excellent results, also.

The practitioner of the Emotion Code and Body Code uses applied kinesiology. This is a holistic technique commonly called "muscle testing." With the client's permission, the practitioner obtains—from the client's subconscious mind— yes or no answers to questions regarding the chosen issue. (The subconscious mind remembers everything we experience). The trapped emotions involved are identified, and their energy is released magnetically. The client's difficulty will disappear or become manageable, or additional session(s) may be required.

Earlier when I said, "See Chapter 5," I was referring to this particular paragraph, here. With muscle testing, I could learn some abuse details which I describe in my personal story. They include my age at the time of the trauma, with whom, when and where the trauma occurred, as well as which trapped emotions and other negative energies need to be released.

With Dr. Nelson's method, I could choose what I wanted to release. I cleared some sexual abuse traumas immediately with the Emotion Code. Eliminating those negative energies from my childhood abuse started to improve my mood, my sexual experiences, and my life in general. It raised my vibrations. I felt lighter and happier. My sexual shame began to dissolve when I released trapped emotions like low self-esteem, helplessness, worthlessness, lack of control, humiliation, and shame.

I also released those self-fulfilling prophecies I mentioned at the beginning of Chapter 1. Dr. Nelson calls them Post Hypnotic Suggestions, a term which highlights their hypnotic quality (they stay with you and show up when you least want them). For example, if I gave a speech or talked in a group, I would hear my father's voice in my head saying, "You don't know what you're talking about" and "Nobody wants to hear what you have to say."

Now, those predictions are released and no longer cause me doubt and confusion when I speak to others. My father could no longer undermine my confidence that way. I actually breathe better since I cleared my mother's proclamation about my not deserving the air I breathe.

I released the energy of those three traumatic events in Chapter 1—my father's abuse, my mother blaming me for what he did, and the meeting where they told me the abuse was my fault. As a result, those memories seem like unfortunate events from the past. They have no emotional impact now. I continued to release my traumas this way.

Between learning the Emotion Code and the Body Code, I dated and married my second husband. We had been friends when we worked at the same agency and were both married to others. A few weeks after his wife's funeral, I called him. Reaching out like that was unusual for me. He had seemed to be a devoted husband, and I thought he could use some support. I was aware he was single now, but I wasn't considering that. He was not my type. We went out to lunch a few times and then a few more times.

After we had spent a lot of time together, I could see this man was my new type of man. He was consistently caring, supportive and loving. I was amazed to find so little trauma and drama in me and in our relationship. This wasn't boring—it was soothing and reassuring to the survivor in me. With time and a lot of testing (by me), I knew he was the man I loved and wanted in my life. He accepted me, unconditionally, with all my baggage. Loving him hurt only a little, infrequently. Some hurt is inevitable in a long term relationship.

A few months before I contacted him, I'd had lunch with an older woman friend who told me she was getting married. I had recently decided I wanted to have someone special in my life, again, if I could find him.

I asked my friend, "How did you do that?'

I didn't expect an answer, but my friend had one. She replied, "I said this prayer: 'God, I would love to have another relationship with a man, but I haven't been good at choosing them. If you want that for me, and I hope you do, I need you to pick him and put him near me, so I'll know he's the one.'"

I wrote down every word. I repeated it in prayer for about three months. Then it happened.

Honest, in-depth, clear communication was, and is, essential for my husband and me. We work at that until we get it. It helps us to get close. My husband was more loving and trusting than I. I watched him and learned from him. He put up with the effects of my trauma; I put up with his unresolved issues.

Although he didn't understand why I would want to do either, he supported my healing work and later my book-writing. That was because they mattered to me. I did some energy healing work for him because he matters to me, and he let me do it. I am more than grateful for our relationship. I taught my husband how to be grateful, too. I appreciate he is willing to admit he learned something from me.

I told him some of my sexual abuse history while feeling vulnerable and cautious. It was difficult to talk about, but I pushed myself to say what I needed to say and to ask questions. That worked out well and made us closer. But I tackled my sexual issues by myself with the Body Code. I wanted to maintain the romance between us while I released my remaining traumas.

Today, I told my love, apologetically, that I had fit him into my book between the Emotion Code and the Body Code. He quipped, "Well, I guess that's better than being between a rock and a hard place." Besides his humor, his foot rubs are good.

With the Body Code system, I worked on the physical, mental, emotional, and spiritual effects of my trauma. I found appropriate medical attention for food allergies, unbalanced hormones, and other issues. My health gradually improved, too.

I worked on my childhood abandonment issues. When I cleared them, I could feel the energy start to move in my body. I felt separate and self-contained in a healthy way. I discovered I had a mean streak toward myself. Ever since childhood, I had unconsciously punished myself for being "bad." It was related to my shame about the abuse, of course.

I eliminated that roadblock so I could work with, not against, myself.

To change my self-perception, I released negative programs and unhealthy energy connections between my parents and me. Also, with the Body Code, I brought parts of my spirit back into my body. One part of my spirit had left me when my mother said she hated me. Then, I finally began to feel I have a place in the world.

Next, I focused on how I felt about other people and how they seemed to experience me. I had been too embarrassed to talk to therapists about my discomfort in social situations. I was ashamed. As a therapist, I should not have that problem. I was still afraid to love and get close to people other than my husband and family, and I was still working on that, too. Keeping people at a distance had made me feel safe but lonely. I felt I was flawed and defective.

Do I want to be closer to people? Do I want more meaningful relationships? Do I dare let go and love others freely and unconditionally? Yes. That is what I want. I released some fear energy.

I had the most difficulty with groups. Fortunately, I was a member of three groups. I watched what I did and felt in our meetings. I noticed when I had an urge to talk, I worried about what people would think if I said what I wanted to say. I censored myself. I couldn't bring up new topics of conversation or share much about myself without high anxiety. Sometimes I would feel that familiar left-out shame and worthlessness I had felt in my childhood at home and at school. Other times I would judge others as unworthy of me! That was another excuse to avoid contact.

I had a flash of insight that went deep. The people I know, now, are not my parents or my sister. These people are not doing what that family did. What I might experience or misinterpret as rejection is my childhood trauma being triggered in the present. I must have an inner child, reacting in me, who needs to be brought up to date.

If I expect and look for my original family rejection, that's what I will see. I will create it in my expectation and then by doing what I always did. My thinking will lead to feeling helpless. Then I won't participate; I will feel left out and sad. Instead, I can bring back and use those parts of myself, such as my loving spirit and the spontaneity and creativity which I abandoned as a child.

It was enlightening to experience a group of innocent people and not react inside as if they were my family of origin. I was shocked and sad when I realized how much baggage I carried around. I was delighted to get rid of some. Now, I see people are just people. They do what they do. They are vulnerable like I am. I should know—I help clients several days a week in my counseling and therapy work. Everyone has bad experiences. Now I'm in the group called humanity instead of being that little person all alone in the world. "Hey, welcome to the world," I say to myself.

I looked in the mirror one day and asked myself, "What do other people see?" My eyes looked tense and frightened. I told my eyes they could relax. They did, for that moment. My birthday is on the cusp of Pisces. I wonder which is the real me—deep thinking and serious, or fun and gregarious Aquarius. It's obvious. Some things probably won't change. When I wanted to work on how other people saw me, I resisted asking anyone for feedback. I was embarrassed. I believed that was something you ask your girlfriends at ten years old when you are becoming socially conscious. I had missed that landmark by quite a few miles. I was stubborn. I preferred to handle it myself and guess.

On second thought, maybe I didn't want to hear the answers, or I didn't want to put other people on the spot and embarrass them, too. All were true.

Since childhood, being safe meant I had to sacrifice positive attention from other people. I didn't want to be seen or heard, but then I would be angry, internally, at other people for not seeing and hearing me. I must have held that against my parents, too. Hmm. That's interesting. Leave me alone/don't leave me alone. Not a good message.

Recently I attended a holistic fair. While I was speaking to one of the proprietors about her services, two women approached her in the middle of our conversation. She turned away from me and talked to them. I waited patiently. What happened? I felt angry and shut out. I didn't think interrupting would work. Eventually I said "screw it" to myself and left.

Later, as I walked by that booth, one of those women stopped me and said, "Didn't you want to buy something here, earlier?"

I told the proprietor, "I felt ignored by you, and I changed my mind."

She replied, "That was not my fault. That was a problem with your energy."

I was shocked at her attitude. I said, "You've got to be kidding. Would you explain that?" Her answer told me nothing.

The proprietor seemed unwilling to look at the part she played in the problem, but I figured this experience could be a gift from the universe. I had received quite a few of those, lately. Maybe she knew something about me I didn't know.

People do ignore me a fair amount. The man selling vegetables on the street two days ago skipped me and waited on the next person in line. When I objected, "Wait a minute! I was next," it made no difference to him. Why? What do I do?

Do I think I am special? No. I think I am especially defective. I realize there is some arrogance in the idea that I am the worst of the worst. Do I still need not to be seen or heard in spite of the work I've done? There must be something else going on. If I am showing in my body language that I don't want to be seen and heard by others, and they are picking up on it, that would explain why people ignore me. I might look like I want—or expect—to be ignored. I think

I understand. That is what I do. I'm still not finished with being invisible.

People who use different methods for healing often agree the healing process is like peeling an onion. As you peel toward the center, you reach the most critical and sensitive issues. These are usually about our worth and lovableness— no matter what happens to us in childhood. I had several of those involving my mother. After my mother died, I continued the power struggle between us by myself. When I needed to do a task, I was alternately the harsh, demanding mother, saying, "You must," and the stubborn child, saying, "You can't make me." Believe, me, it was difficult to get anything done that way.

Recently, I heard that little child voice in my head say, "*I could be much more cooperative if you would just ask me nicely.*"

My adult-self replied, "Duh, why didn't I think of that?" Since then, these two parts of me have been working together quite nicely.

Here's another way my mother was still in my life long after she passed. When we were little, my parents occasionally took my sister and me to a Hungarian restaurant for dinner. I liked the place and especially the beautiful sound of the cimbalom music they played for the diners. I remember the servers were especially kind to children and were patient while I decided what to eat. On one of our visits, I was four years old, and we were celebrating my father's birthday.

On my way back from my solo trip to the restroom, a man and woman sitting at a table near my path started a conversation with me. They asked me questions and listened to what I said. They seemed enchanted with me in the same way that I am, now, with cute children I see in restaurants. We talked and laughed. I was comfortable and spontaneous while soaking up their warm, friendly attention. This was a new experience for me.

My mother came to get me. She looked upset. Back at our table, she was furious, sporting her angry frown and bulgy eyes, again. Her whisper sounded like hissing. "You should never talk to strangers. What's the matter with you? Terrible things could happen to you. How could you do that? You should know better."

"They didn't hurt me," I protested. "Those people were nice."

My father and sister looked at their plates and said nothing. Was it because they knew if they spoke, her anger would escalate? I felt they didn't care about me. Neither parent attempted to protect me from the rage of the other.

Then, my mother, with her twisted face and maximum contempt in her voice, said, "Your zipper is unzipped. I'm so embarrassed. You should be ashamed of yourself for being exposed like that in public. You are so careless. What kind of mother will people think I am?"

I didn't know she was ridiculous. Neither my father nor my sister commented on her attitude or behavior. My mother was unconcerned about my feelings or her behavior. Soon, it was as if this event had never happened—for them. But I felt deflated, tiny, and worthless. Looking back, I realize that, instead of being angry at my mother, I stopped liking the restaurant. It wasn't special anymore. That was a big disappointment.

The effects of this trauma showed up later. As an adult, when I was alone after I'd had a good time with friends, I would have painful feelings and thoughts. I would say to myself, "I have undoubtedly said or done something terribly wrong that I don't know about." I would feel a lot of shame and try to figure out what I did or said that was inappropriate or offensive. Finally, I traced those feelings back to this early childhood incident. Nothing I had done was inappropriate. This reaction was an echo of the past. That's where I got my excessive fear of saying or doing the wrong thing, a fear that plagued me most of my life.

Sometimes I look for the big picture and the symbolism behind the symptoms. One of the big issues I resolved was my discovery that since childhood, I had resisted taking anything into my body and letting anything out. The act of taking something in symbolized accepting parental stuff I didn't want, such as their criticism, abuse, anger, and neglect. It included resistance to taking in other people—their ideas, personalities, differences from me, their compliments, or even their love, sometimes.

Letting things out represented loss, like losing Angel or parts of myself I was forced to give up. In my childhood, this was a way I could exercise some control over myself and my life without my parents' interference.

This conflict showed up, as an adult, in difficulties with my eating, digestion, and excretion. I didn't have an eating disorder. I just didn't like to eat. Some of that related to being forced to eat those vegetables I hated as a child. I released all the above with the Body Code. That all works well now.

REFLECTIONS

Presently, I am outgoing sometimes. I'm a clam in a shell at other times. My second husband tells me I am lots more outgoing. He is encouraging and pleased for me that I'm reaching my goals. Clearly, now, I am more available to him and other people. I'm no longer in a hurry to escape from social situations. I participate more, and I like them. My hostility toward my parents and other abusers, which bled onto everyone else I met, is defused. Each person I meet is, indeed, a new person, not a potential abuser or a replica of an abuser. I am less eager to judge and more open to see and hear and appreciate other people. I am more relaxed, and free to enjoy them.

CHAPTER 6

Speaking out,
the Incest Plague,

Facing Truths

After I had cleared most of the trauma and what I wanted
to change about myself, I felt so much better. I wanted to
write about my life. Actually, my friend was writing a book.
It sounded intriguing. I had only written short reports and
term papers in college. I decided to do it.

Since I've given myself permission to speak, I am driven to
write. As a child, the only person I told about what happened
to me was my mother—and you know that didn't work.
Eventually, I talked about my abuse with therapists, but I
left out the painful details. I'm breaking my dysfunctional
family, and our societal rules left and right, now. I blush when
I tell someone the subject of my book is incest. This topic is
taboo. Let's talk about it.

Do you know research indicates that 97% of reported cases of incest involve little girls? Can you believe one in 20 in-tact families and 1 in 7 blended families (with female children) engage in father-daughter incest. This, of course, would be instigated by the father on the little girl(s) living under his roof. Then there are uncles, cousins, and women who abuse. Incest is rampant. First, we need to be aware; then we need to care. Women's rights start at birth.

Since these little girls were forced to give up control of their bodies as children, they become women who are unable to defend themselves against men or don't know abuse when they see it. Or, they believe abuse is all they deserve in a relationship. What they need is corrective emotional experiences with love. Instead, they are likely to volunteer themselves or be forced into situations like domestic violence, prostitution, and human trafficking. They are vulnerable to addictions, which promise to soothe both past and present pain.

I want to help increase worldwide awareness of the devastating effects of incest on the victim. I want to help stop what happened to me from happening to other children. Incest is tragic and traumatic. It takes decades or a lifetime to recover. For many victims, access to help is not available or affordable. They don't get relief.

Only 30% of father/daughter incest victims report the crime. Those who do report need support in that process from sensitive, trained people who receive and act on the information appropriately. I believe that is happening with hotline calls, at least.

Perpetrators need to be prosecuted and taught to refrain from doing what they are driven to do. They need to learn how and why sexual abuse hurts because they were traumatized, also.

Since I started writing this book, I've received a lot of help from higher sources. It must be the right thing for me to do. *Thanks for the support. I need it.*

The universe brought me another writing friend. We meet weekly to read our unfinished books to each other and talk about our progress. This friend experienced a close and satisfying relationship with her sister. She asked me, "What was wrong between you and your sister?"

I said, "I don't know. My sister was always aloof toward me. I don't know why she ignored me."

My friend suggested, "You can have a good, a bad, or an in-between relationship with your sister. It's not normal to have nothing going on with your sister. What was the reason for that?"

I told her I thought my father had stopped abusing my sister around age six to appease my mother. His abuse of me became worse then. My friend said, "That's it. That's why your sister ignored you. She was relieved she didn't have to tolerate your father's abuse. She felt guilty. If she thought you were a terrible person, she could say to herself, 'My sister deserves what she gets.'"

That was already my mother's attitude. If they discussed it, my mother would reinforce my sister's story about me.

I told my writing friend about an assignment in Family Dynamics class for my master's degree in counseling. We were to ask a family member his or her opinion of some aspect of the behavior in our family of origin. It was a simple, non-intrusive question, but my sister had refused to help me with the assignment. Finally, I said to her, "You are the only one of the family who is still living. You must help me. The teacher has refused to accept 'nothing' for my homework assignment. I already asked her."

My sister agreed reluctantly. A week later, I received her response in the mail. In a few short sentences, she said something like, "We all got along pretty well." The note ended in mid-sentence. It wasn't like her to be sloppy or careless.

After the conversation with my friend, my brain was still absorbing what she said. I could remember my sister's attitude of disgust toward me. It appears that "nobody loved me" was a true statement, not just the feeling I had. My muscle testing validated that information. My sister felt guilty and blamed me. My truth-seeking self was satisfied, but the rest of me was depressed.

If my sister and I had talked and shared our abuse experiences and pain, this might have been a different, warmer story. My life might have been a warmer life. With one ally, I could believe other people could be allies, too. I wouldn't have been so alone.

In a family, when the alliance between the two adults isn't working, an unhealthy relationship can develop between a parent and child. We had two of those. I got the one that was left over. My mother and sister met each other's emotional needs, so my sister didn't need to relate to me.

As adults, my sister and I had contact on occasions when we visited my father and stepmother at the same time. When my sister's nearly-grown son was terminally ill, I asked myself what a real sister would do. I called her to offer emotional support. We decided to meet half-way between our two different states. We continued to meet at least yearly for more than ten years. When I re-married, we brought our husbands. They often came to our house for Thanksgiving. But if I talked about anything important or personal, my sister showed little interest. She didn't work. She didn't want to hear about my work. She didn't have interests, or do anything for fun. She couldn't make up her mind about anything. I received more enthusiastic responses from strangers. She did show some concern for me during my divorce.

She refused to discuss our past. I know she had blamed me for the family problems and my mother's stress—maybe even her early death. She would say, "I wish I had helped her more." I believe I was supposed to jump on that and take more responsibility for not helping enough. I didn't.

I had no success in steering the conversation to the sexual abuse place. I was afraid to just come out with it. Instead, I decided that some relationship with my sister was better than nothing. But it really wasn't. It was nothing.

My sister seemed to me like a shell of a person long before she got dementia. I guess that's how I would have been, without all the help I received.

I had quite a few "almost" relationships in my life—my father, my sister, my first husband, and the boyfriend who cheated on me. I saw the potential of the "almosts." Most of those people gave me some attention, but they didn't love me or have my back. I didn't choose people well when I had a choice. I didn't expect proper treatment. Those people gave me the false hope I needed to keep going. I honored the *don't tell* rule about my abuse. I think the true reason was my mighty shame and how terrible I would feel afterward if I told someone. At that time I still secretly felt it was my fault.

Now, I own who I am. I believe in myself. I share more. I give more. I receive better. I don't hang on to poor relationships. It's more comfortable—though still embarrassing—to talk about my abuse and neglect. I have to practice saying the word "incest" to other people. When I told my card-playing group about my book, I blushed, dissociated, and couldn't pay attention to the cards afterward. I need more practice with that.

While I was writing this book, a particular thought about my mother kept returning. I'd had it before and pushed it away. I muscle tested it several times. I wanted to be wrong, but it was a "yes" every time. This is what was surfacing:

After I was born and she took me home from the hospital, my mother attempted to drown me in the kitchen sink during a bath. My father walked in and stopped her. I thought, *if this is really true, I will have trapped emotions all over my body from this event.* I did. They made sense for the situation. Terror and horror were among those I released.

I decided I would leave this attempt to drown out of my book. It's too sensational. People will think I'm making it up and will doubt what I say. Then I thought, *Well, whose story is this anyway?* I know what happened. I remember my mother telling me she tried to drown me. I was about five years old then. That was one of those statements she could make that caused me to feel as bad as she did.

There's a saying I've heard: "You never forgive the one you hurt." Every time she had to look at me, did it remind her she tried to drown me? My muscle testing says "yes." Is that why she hated me? "Yes." That was one reason. Was I isolated from the family so I would be kept away from my mother? Yes. Why didn't they banish her, instead of me? No answer. Now I understand why my father was willing to pay for maids to take care of me after I was born.

Those resulting trapped emotions and psychic traumas were all over my body—in my circuits, systems, organs, glands, chakras, everywhere. I must have been close to drowning. *So that's why I had trouble breathing when I swam.*

119

It's a panicky feeling that I wouldn't get enough air. I released all of it with the Body Code. Now, I love swimming and everything else that takes place in water. Deep water doesn't scare me. It's a great place to go to be alone.

It's interesting how new information can alter what I thought was a reality. Being sure of anything about someone else is unwise. I no doubt have fooled myself and missed more that should have been evident. For example, I was surprised when I realized my father had helped my mother in ways I had never noticed as a child. He was her husband, doctor, and nurturer. To my knowledge, she confided only in my sister and complained about her aches and pains to my father.

Now, I realize, my father attended, frequently, to both her physical and mental problems. She was sick, worried, anxious or depressed most of the time. He listened to her complaints when he was home. He doctored and medicated her. He occasionally took her to specialists. My father drove my mother to the grocery store and everywhere else she went. No one else helped her. This was something I saw him do as I grew up. I didn't think of the time and energy it cost him along with his job and other activities. No wonder he didn't want to drive me anywhere. He didn't tell me why—or maybe he did, and I failed to understand.

Yet he was a philanderer, which caused my mother intense suffering. A strange conversation at my mother's funeral made me wonder if my father had maintained the affair for twenty years that he was having when I was born. My boyfriend's mother, whom I hadn't met before, asked me—in front of the other people at the buffet table, believe it or not—"Is your father going to marry _____ now?"

I said, "What?"

When she realized I didn't know what she was talking about, and someone nearby hushed her, she mumbled and changed the subject. My father didn't marry that other woman. He married a new "other woman."

While writing this book, I suddenly understood what should have been evident to me as a therapist. I had been in complete denial. *My mother was mentally ill.* They covered it up and blamed her symptoms on her heart disease and me while they promoted the wonderful mother myth. My father did not complain or tell my sister and me what was wrong.

Let's see: My mother tried to drown me as a new-born, and it seems, at the time, she knew what she was doing. Periodically she threatened to kill herself. She made one scary suicide attempt in front of us—she jumped into deep water without knowing how to swim. Then she changed her mind and was rescued.

Apparently, one of the hospitalizations was due to another suicide attempt and depression. My mother would say. "You're going to give me a nervous breakdown if you don't do, or stop doing, such and such." She was mentally unstable in my presence. I believe she was suffering from her childhood trauma, and more.

If you know your mother is mentally ill, you don't expect normalcy from her. That doesn't make it easy, but it's easier to live with if you are not blamed for her problems. The family myth that she was a terrific mother with a heart problem was a total denial of me and my reality.

My father had to know better, but my sister and I did not. In those days, mental illness was viewed as a bigger disgrace than it is now. At least her illness could have been acknowledged when we were adults.

I decided to release the trauma around my birth with the Body Code. It was a rough delivery for both of us. Some of my trapped emotions I released were abandonment, anxiety, overwhelm, vulnerability, lack of control, and unworthy. All of these were inherited by me from my mother. They went back three generations in her family.

I was unprepared for this emotional jolt. I learned, for three generations, the women in my mother's family had hated their daughters. Then I discovered why. During that same time, the fathers were incestuously abusing those daughters. I muscle tested this several times. I always got the same answers.

My poor mother. Family members from two generations before her were steeped in incest family behavior and training. She inherited their negative feelings and lived with those of other family members, too. Her father and her older brother molested her. She had no fresh air.

I just visualized the picture of that rocking chair in my grandfather's house where I remember, now, he molested me—only one time, I think. Now I see why my memory of him was so foggy. I had remembered my grandmother, but I had succeeded in forgetting him. Now I know why.

Under those circumstances, how could my mother have been any different from what she was? Those feelings and behaviors are passed down. They become wide-spread and "acceptable" throughout the family. How could she have learned how to parent with both a hostile mother and grandmother? How could she have known how to avoid marrying a perpetrator?

I feel differently about my mother now. I feel more compassion and sadness for her. So many things she did and said make sense now. I see why she was so angry, anxious, scared, desperate, and worried. She couldn't look at me because she saw the worst of herself in me. She couldn't tolerate seeing me or my pain because what she saw was her pain. I get it.

I'm exhausted. How are you? This must be difficult for the reader. Sharing my story now is more important than ever. I want people to understand not only the consequences of incest for the survivor but also that it must not be continually passed down to future generations. Passing it down creates endless numbers of victims!

After lots of perfectionistic editing, I had finished my first three chapters. One day I was reading Chapter 1 for the umpteenth time. As a beginning writer, I learned first chapters are vitally important. They set the tone of the book and tell you about the writer. I asked myself, "How does this first chapter sound?" What would someone else notice here? There's a flavor of something all over this first page. It isn't vanilla chocolate or strawberry.

I read that chapter again. I see my history. I couldn't stick up for myself as a child or change anything in my family. There's a sense of helplessness there. That belongs on the page. My childhood never ended. The actual incest and neglect were finished decades ago, but the effects of it stayed on in my body, brain, and spirit for most of my life. I had defects in my writing from life avoidance.

What is the feeling behind my writing? Oh, I think I'm feeling sorry for myself. That's it. I feel sorry for myself in the past for having had to live through that and for myself in the present, for having had a past like that. I have certainly earned the right to feel sorry for myself—but do I want to do that?

During the first few years of my sex abuse healing, I felt like a victim. I could see it in myself, and in some of my clients, as well. I had learned that I could get stuck in that position. If I defined myself as a victim, there was no way out. That's why "survivor" is such an important word. I had no power or choice as a child. I have some as an adult.

I purposely gave up feeling like a victim, or I thought I did. This must be a milder version of victimhood.

When I started writing my story, I, who rarely trusted myself, assumed I could write a decent book with a satisfying ending. I had no idea what it would be. I'm not at the end yet, but at this moment, I have achieved an enormous benefit. I just now saw what I've been doing, so now I can stop doing it. I can stop feeling sorry for myself. It's not helpful. I choose to feel relief and appreciation instead. That's a promise to me. It gives me chills all over.

Although I didn't realize I was feeling sorry for myself before this, I had noticed I thought a lot of negative thoughts. Some people call them ANTS—Automatic Negative Thoughts. I've been reading and hearing for years that we can alter our brains and change the way we think. Scientists have discovered brain plasticity, which means our brains can change. I was sure I couldn't eliminate my negative thoughts— not me, with all that overactivity.

I decided to notice how those negative thoughts made me feel. *Bad*. They made me feel bad. They were excessive and unnecessary. This automatic negative thinking was not compatible with my healing goal.

What if I tried cutting off every negative thought I noticed coming into my mind to see what happens? New negative thoughts may need my attention, but very few of them are new. I said, *"stop"* loudly in my head. I noticed the ANTS left but immediately trouped back into my brain. The ANTS continued to rule. I kept saying, "stop." Eventually, I had fewer negative thoughts. Then, I added another requirement. How about replacing the ANTS with loving or grateful thoughts? My negative side said, "Oh, give me a break," but sometimes I do replace them.

Now, I hardly notice any ANTS at all. If I spot them, I usually can send them away immediately. My mind is freer. I feel peaceful. I love it.

Having a lot of negative thoughts implies that they show up, and I have no control over them. *Doing a lot of negative thinking* says I'm making them happen or letting them happen. The last statement is the true one. I can create a different mindset. I can create a new reality. The world is what we make it.

I made another powerful change in my thinking, recently. I stopped trying to be in control of anything or anyone other than myself. It's too stressful trying to be in charge of other people, events or whether my plane crashes with me in it (unless I'm the pilot). Trying to be in control when you aren't doesn't work. It creates a lot of unnecessary stress. Before this, I was a frequent control freak. I like to help other people, but I'm not in charge of their choices.

I taught myself not to judge events as either good or bad. Whatever happens, is what happens. It is what it is. My job is to decide what I need to do about what happened or changed. I'm comfortable in the world this way.

I don't expect things to go the way I think they should. They either will or they won't. I leave the possibility open that the outcome could be better than the one I had hoped for. Or not. Either way, usually, something good comes out of the bad.

While I was writing these words, I had a call from a former client whose new problem is a tragic loss. It was so sad to hear. That reminds me to say, you may have to wait sometimes to find the positive side of a change.

It's interesting to watch how things turn out, to choose my own behavior and look for solutions when things happen unexpectedly. I trust in the universe. It does seem to have my back. I have been noticing a lot of support, lately. The more I am grateful, the more I can trust and the more help I get.

Many years ago, I read this line at an Al-anon meeting: Everything is exactly the way it's supposed to be. I said to myself, at the time, "The person who came up with that is out of his mind. Things should be how I want them to be." Really?

Now, I believe that Al-anon saying. It's become a comforting thought. I don't need to try to be in charge. It's like going with the flow. I picture a stream.

My very first change in thinking occurred when I was in a college psychology class. I learned I was a negative thinker and reactor. Just like my mother, I saw the negative side of things first and foremost. Something was not just troublesome— it was a catastrophe. I decided to try to change the imbalance.

When I noticed my cynical view, I searched for the positive. Now, I see both sides, with the emphasis being on the positive a lot of the time. It feels good. It took me six months to make that adjustment to my thinking.

I gave up another version of negative thinking I call "hash and re-hash." For example, I did a poor job of selling my house after my divorce. I made lousy decisions during a period of grief and stress. I failed to ask for help or support when I needed it, and I lost a lot of profit in the sale. This was an opportunity to make extra money going into my single life and a one-time chance for financial security. I had good reason to be disgusted with myself when I realized what I had done.

For years, I harassed myself over my faulty judgment. I couldn't undo it, forgive myself, or let it go. I would hash over the whole situation, periodically, question every detail and feel much worse afterward.

Finally, when I saw I was starting to do that, I said to myself, "Stop. Stop right now. Don't go there. You know what happens when you do. Nothing has changed. There's no new information. I have explored every possibility of what I could have done differently. I've learned everything I needed to learn. I can't change it now. You know when you do this, you end up feeling terrible and depressed and much worse afterward. Let it go!"

Later, I shortened the speech to "Don't go there—you know how it makes you feel." This took some time, maybe six months, but it worked. I rarely think about that money loss. I give myself the short talk if I do.

I have many fewer negative thoughts about myself now. I don't hear, "I'm a terrible person" anymore. I am less critical of others. I don't think about how they "should be," like I sometimes did. Honestly, I used to think people should be more like me. Ha!

If I get stressed, my reaction can deteriorate. But it won't likely be some situation over which I think I should have control or a past circumstance that turned out badly which I replay over and over in my head. It won't be because I see practically everything in a negative light. Because I don't—not anymore. I'm in charge of my brain. Congratulations to me and thank you for listening.

This is my motto to myself: I am responsible for everything I think and say to myself. I reject the negativity gently. I'm going to keep my first chapter as it is because that's how I felt at the time I wrote it. I see I've made some significant progress. It took some work and perseverance to change my mind. That's important to my health and happiness. I have actually changed my brain.

I started a gratitude practice. I had heard it was a great thing to do for your mental health and spirituality, but even so, I began it reluctantly. I didn't expect much. When I drove to work in the morning, I would state everything I could think of for which I was, or could be, grateful.

At first, doing my assignment was mechanical and tedious. After some time passed, I noticed if I felt terrible when I started, I would feel better when I finished. If I already felt good, I would feel better yet.

The results of my gratitude expressions were excellent over time. I noticed more in my life to appreciate—a flower, a bug, a smile. I became more alive to my senses and my sense of pleasure. I agree, now, with the people who say the universe brings you more of what you focus on. When you appreciate what you have, it brings you more to appreciate. A lot of it is delightful, small stuff, but taken all together, they are significant. I'm grateful that I'm grateful. I love it.

REFLECTIONS

Sparkles

I'm going to work. I back my car out of the garage. The old garage door grinds its way to the ground. The house looks so pretty in the sun with the snow all around it. Everything sparkles. The streets are already cleared.

As usual, we just drank our morning coffee together, my husband and I. He sat in the old rocker that came with me and the house. I sat across from him on our red love seat. Coffee time was special today. We sparkle, too, with the right conditions. His sense of humor is delightful.

I've always been serious and analytical. I wonder what my husband does that makes him funny, so, naturally, I analyze it. He takes something that is actually a problem with his thinking (worrying too much) to the extreme. He makes a cute little story and exaggerates the worst that could happen in the current circumstances. Everybody laughs because it's funny, and we all catastrophize and exaggerate, sometimes. It fascinates me how he takes the worst and makes something good out of it. He benefits, and people like him for his sense of humor.

My car is so new, I love seeing it look pretty and clean. I washed it in mid-winter in the driveway because the last snow made it look so messy. This snow scene, today, is magic. I'm overwhelmed with the abundance in my life. My body feels open and relaxed. I thank God and the universe.

As I drive to work, some negativity creeps into my thoughts. What's this? It is a familiar theme. I feel vulnerable. If I get too comfortable, or too happy, someone will knock me down. I remind myself that although it used to be that way, it's not likely to happen now. I'm safe.

Moments change. Everything changes. It feels good to live in the present and catch the next moment—whatever it brings. Today, I passed the test for accepting what comes.

CHAPTER 7

Achieving Insight and Freedom

Now I know how wonderful feeling great can be. What I wanted was emotional pain relief. I achieved so much more. I know what it's like to have a sense of myself as a whole person. I'm freer to be myself and to care about others.

Changing my thinking was the final challenge of my healing. I waited so long—I didn't think it was possible. I didn't realize how much work I had done until I saw it on paper. My mind is less cluttered. That feels good. I'm pleased with myself for my progress and surprised that it was possible.

I want to say more about what was exceptional about my childhood and me. Again, I'm thankful for the following: food, clothing, shelter, nice home, excellent school, college education. I'm grateful I could get the therapy I needed later on when I was married.

As a child, I was sheltered from what transpired in the world. I didn't know what other people suffered or that they did suffer. If I had, perhaps that would have given me some perspective on my situation.

One of my long-term clients told me there was only one thing wrong with me as a therapist: I didn't know what it was like to be poor. I didn't tell her this. She just knew. I love feedback and I was pleased she took the risk of saying that. I said, "Thank you for telling me that, and it's true." Then I asked her, "What is it like for you to be poor?" She told me. I listened carefully.

Here's what I think is exceptional about me. I survived. I made a good life for myself in spite of my history. I married and raised children, and had a decent job. I looked better than I felt. Then my life fell apart with my divorce.

While grieving, I started from scratch and re-created myself. I learned to define and achieve what I wanted. I risked letting other people teach me and support me. In choosing to face my hurt, I encouraged myself to allow and feel the pain so I could lose the pain. It was well worth it.

Digging into the sexual abuse work was never easy. In the beginning, some of my feelings were still shut down; a lot of survivors start out in therapy that way. Obtaining information about sexual abuse stirs you up and gets you in touch with yourself. I read many books about sex abuse at that time. I dealt with my fear while enjoying the opportunity to explore my sexuality.

Here's a bit of a poem I love, comparing the experience of personal growth to frozen rivers thawing in the spring.

Mary E. Mebane wrote *On Change*, "At the end of the cracking, breaking, violent period, the river is open, life-giving, life-caring."

I think I'm doing well in the sociability department. I watch other women being friends. I see what it's like and what they do. I'm watching other people handle relationships, and helping them when they are my clients or friends. I'm less focused on myself and more interested in relating now. I've moved up from loner to introvert status. I'll probably always be one of those. They say you can't change from introvert to extrovert. Ha. We'll see.

Here is what I learned, recently:

- Changing my thoughts can change my brain, which can change my life.
- Significant improvements in my sociability occurred when I discovered how I had allowed my past history to affect the present, and expected poor treatment from innocent people. Then I was able to change the pattern of my relating. I get more involved. I feel safer now.
- If I indulge in feeling sorry for myself about what happened in my childhood, I will depress myself. A direct trigger to feeling miserable is, "I don't deserve this. It shouldn't have happened to me." That's true, of course, and most survivors feel that way in the beginning. It's important to feel your emotions, but that's a good one to let go.

- The most surprising truth I learned while writing this book was that my father was not the only major problem in my childhood. For years, I put all the responsibility for my pain, shame, and anger on him and his sexual and emotional abuse. Yes, he was an incest perpetrator/rapist. That was horrendous. That was about my being used to meet someone else's needs. He had no concern for my needs, but his abuse implied I had some value.

Meanwhile, I had thoroughly minimized the impact of my mother's hateful attitude and lack of love. Her words and actions sent a powerful message to me: "You don't matter. You are worthless." I had discounted her behavior, partly because she wasn't as scary or physically threatening as my father.

Actually, my mother's behavior was as damaging as my father's behavior. I had thought I didn't take her personally, but I was deceiving myself and minimizing the results. I did take what she did and said personally. She was my mother. I had many painful memories of her, which affected my self-esteem and my ability to function. I felt I should never do anything better than she did. She'd be mad or hurt. Also, I inherited many of her trapped emotions, so I actually felt her feelings along with mine.

With the truth out in the open, I could feel it, grieve it and accept it, finally. I'm a little raw, yet. Here's the most important thing I learned. My mother hated me because that's what happened in previous generations in her family of origin. She was the only daughter in the family. They abused her and passed the abuse and neglect down to her, and then she passed it down to me, the second girl in our family. The first child in all our families was the family "hero." My own second child inherited many of the trapped emotions about my abuse and some that I inherited from my mother.

As inadequate as my mother was in protecting me, I realize now that I had convinced myself she would keep me safe if I were in severe danger from my father. I know this because when I heard the news my mother had died, I began to shake. I shook for an hour, without knowing why. I quizzed myself and I asked a few other people: "In what condition having to do with a family member's death does a person shake?" Grief, sadness, or my sense of relief didn't require shaking.

I wasn't aware of feeling any of those, except the sense of relief. Anger was a possibility, but it wasn't anger, either. It was fear. My mother's protection was gone. I was twenty-one years old, but my inner child self was shaking for her life.

Motherhood. It's the most important job. Nobody is quite good enough for that responsibility. Everything I learned from this healing process made me a better mother. When I started, I had a long way to go. I wasn't present enough for my children. I didn't teach them basic skills, like how to get ready for school, because I never learned them myself and didn't know they were supposed to be taught. I was preoccupied with myself and my trauma and pain, as an adult, even when I wasn't consciously thinking about it.

Changes came better late than never. When a new awareness would enrich my relationship with my children, I always wished I had known it sooner. My children have been affected by my limitations, and they have observed and admired my courage and perseverance.

As my freedom from trauma increased, my relationships with my children, grandchildren and my second husband's family improved. I was more emotionally present and comfortable with them. I shared more of myself, and they did too. I appreciated them more. As a therapist, I enjoyed doing family therapy with willing families. As you might guess, they taught me, as well.

I haven't included my children in this story because I don't want to mix them up in it. They are another story. My children are beautiful and exceptional people, and they're individual in the ways they show it. I love them so much. Even so, there is a rift in our family. Two people don't talk to each other. It's due to our family dysfunction. Maybe it's something that was passed down from my family or my ex-husband's family. All I know is that I am sad about it, and I can't fix it. I've tried, but it's up to them. It's our own elephant in the living room.

My children know the basics of my history, but not many details. They will decide if they want to read this book. I wish I didn't have to put them in this position. They will have an open invitation to share their reactions, ask questions, cry over it, or whatever needs to be done.

I apologize to any readers who wished to read about confronting the abuser or reporting their abuse to authorities. I had no personal experience with either of these. As a therapist, I have helped clients come to a decision about confronting and reporting after they shared their stories with me. Plans must be made with consideration of individual circumstances

We all know memory can be faulty or distorted. This story is the truth as I recall it and as I discovered it through understanding it in a new way, as well as through muscle testing. Is there more I don't yet know that would change my viewpoint? Maybe.

What prejudices, assumptions and faulty thinking could have distorted my memory? I can't answer those questions, except to say that I have watched for errors and dealt with them when I saw them. It's always been important to me to tell the truth. There is no one living who could corroborate my information.

The reader may doubt my ability to remember. I describe myself in childhood as foggy and dissociative and forgetful of blocks of time. Those are symptoms of sexual abuse. We know sexual abuse memories, while sometimes vivid, can also be scanty. They can leave room for victims to wonder or fill in the blanks. At times, their filling in could be quite intuitive and on the mark. Other times, not.

If memories could be clear, I'm sure most of us would choose that option and get it all over with sooner. But it doesn't work that way. If you have memory issues with childhood sexual abuse, they have to be acknowledged as part of the picture of sexual abuse, in general. Because those memories are traumatic and painful, our bodies and brains try to find ways for us to avoid the pain. That is not a reason to discount the victim's story. No need to blame the victim for that.

The usual problem with the potential of false memories is determining whether the abused person is trying to hurt an innocent party. That happens much less frequently than a perpetrator trying to get away with what he did. That happens in every case—whether the abuser is guilty or not, he denies it; in most cases, it's a false denial. That's why we have the courts to sort that out.

Some people may believe that therapists suggested certain memories or implanted them in my brain. They did not. They waited patiently for me to tell them what happened.

Some people may doubt the validity of the muscle testing I used. Many alternative healers use it successfully. It's uncanny what you can learn. Some people doubt that energy healing works. The method I use produces good results. (Any energy healing is not a substitute for medical treatment.)

My original personal life goal was to feel *better*. As I saw what I did was working, I raised my goal to feel *good*—then to feel *great*. As a child, I had given up my point of view so I could be sure my parents would take care of me. I sacrificed what I knew, along with my individuality, imagination, and spontaneity. Recently, I've been watching those qualities return. *Welcome back.*

Just today, I saw my childhood incest/emotional abuse picture differently. What if my parents hadn't blamed me for what they did? Then I would have seen their abuse as something monstrous they had created and controlled themselves.

Instead, they gave me a false sense of control by telling me that everything wrong was my fault. The way that message affected me was to make me think if I changed myself to perfect, I could change my life. That generated a lifelong incentive for self-improvement.

I often ask myself, "What was my part?" The voice in my head questions me as I write. How much did I contribute to the misery and the drama in the family?

Some people will say I was the way I was because of the terrible things that were done to me. That is true, of course, but my actions and reactions also influenced the actions and reactions of the others.

What was I like as an infant? Was I a happy, smiling, gurgling baby? Probably not. What happens to you early in life when a series of catastrophic events occur with no one dedicated to your care? I must have developed a thick coat of armor to keep people away. Did I act like I wanted anyone to hold me? Did anyone want to? How safe would I have felt I if they did?

Did I miss the best parts of my life because I was overwhelmed by the trauma? Probably. Did I miss opportunities for fun, friends, and connections to others? Sure. I was mildly passive-aggressive, resistant to authority and uncooperative. I was lucky to survive—if you call that luck.

I just realized something else. My larger-than-life view of my parents as powerful, demanding, and rejecting, and myself as powerless and helpless, never changed as I grew up. As an adult, when I thought about my parents, it was a flashback to those traumas in which I am a helpless child. Those traumas were isolated from the rest of me. They did not grow up with the rest of me.

Who was right—them, or me? Were the sexual abuse and emotional neglect my fault? I needed to freshen-up my childlike opinions and perceptions. That happened quite suddenly. I felt like a child two days ago, partially grown up yesterday, and then fully grown up today, all of this within another dimension—the present—where I'm writing and growing older every moment.

I felt sick. I felt nauseated. I realized it's not about how bad my childhood was, or what my parents did, or who was to blame. Although I took some responsibility for my part, I have blamed my parents and sister for what I thought were their parts.

In a way, most of this information is not really significant, but it was the path I needed to take to reach this place. It's not what happens to you that matters. It's what you make of what happens to you that matters. I know that. I have known that for a long time.

The answer I needed was in those pockets of trauma that were tucked away to protect me from the pain. That's why nothing I did or learned as an adult could change my perception. Those parts of me needed to grow up before I could let my parents go emotionally. Then I could release myself from my family's blame and shame. I could do that, myself! Well, how about that? I'm ecstatic.

I couldn't sleep last night. I saw my belief, for the first time, that I couldn't let go of my parents because nobody else would love me. I was despicable—because the sexual abuse had felt good, sometimes, and I blamed myself for that. I thought no one else could or would or should love me. I'm unlovable. I'm ruined. Besides, if your mother didn't love you, no one else will.

At last, those child parts of me felt heard and understood. They integrated with the rest of me. I took some deep breaths.

Over the next few days, I began to feel loveable for the first time. Of course, I'm loveable. Why wouldn't I be? I love my imperfect self. Other people love me, too. I understand the family I grew up in. Now, all that abuse is really over. I feel better, and I can enjoy my life so much more. I can love it. What a relief. *Free. At. Last.* I enjoyed that energy for a few days.

I told my first writing friend—the one who has finished her book—that I am nearly done with mine. She asked, "What about forgiveness? You must include that."

"Oh, yeah, what about forgiveness?" Well, here's what I think: We don't forgive to let the other person off the hook. We forgive so we can be more comfortable with ourselves, and get over the pain of what happened. That's fine. But, to me, forgiving is for the people you love, who love you in return but have hurt you and regret it. We should forgive them. We should forgive frequently, but watch out for people who would take advantage of that and continue to do the same thing. My family of origin didn't seem to know or care that they hurt me. They ignored, disrespected, and demeaned me, and then claimed that I deserved it.

I have forgiven myself. I'm part of the world now, which is brand new to me. Our world is full of suffering, and I want to practice being happy and adding happiness to the world while I can. What I can't promise to forgive, right now, I have let go. I have let go of my mother, father, and sister. My feelings about them are neutral. As for the fact that none of them said goodbye to me, I do have a little grudge about that. But I can say goodbye to them, and especially to my childhood view of them.

Goodbye.

Did anyone owe me a better life? Nothing is guaranteed. There are plenty of lives out there worse than mine. I'm done with the past, as far as I know. I'm comfortable visiting there.

I am the one controlling my present and future life—along with my higher power. I belong to my higher power, the universe, myself, and other people I choose. I belong to the world, which I hope will continue to use me.

This is what I need to tell the world: I grew up in the kind of home in which incest was never expected to happen, so I know it can be perpetrated anywhere by anybody. As already noted, if you are the child victim of ongoing sexual events, incest and your safety become the focus of your life. That is true, even if you have repressed and dissociated most of your memories. The sexual abuse is automatically physical, spiritual and emotional abuse, also. The worst results could be that you can no longer freely give and receive love or experience joy and connection with others. It can ruin you for sex or ruin sex for you. Incest causes you to replace your real self, which is full of shame and must be hidden in secrecy wirh a false self, or acted out in destructive behavior. There is no immediate relief or escape if there is no one to make it stop.

After I had hedged about forgiveness, I continued to think about it. I have studied various approaches to forgiveness for years. I wondered if I was asking too little of myself. Could I be leaving my options open, in case I need to blame someone or excuse myself from something? If I want to hang on to my parents, perhaps I can think of some good memories. The difficulty with forgiving lies in the fact that my parents knew they could ruin my life, and they did what they did, anyway.

Someone recently explained to me that I could forgive that, too. Okay... I'm working on it.

Again, I need to say that something out there helped me write this book. When I needed help, it was there. When I needed emotional support and a different point of view, it was there. When I needed incest information for my book, it showed up in my mailbox. I feel blessed, and I'm grateful. The more grateful I am, the more help I get from the universe and the angels.

And my husband—he loves and supports me and listens and encourages me. I wouldn't have had the freedom or opportunity to write this without him. He supplied me with loads of printer ink and computer paper before I needed it. That simple act made me feel supported. He tolerated the many hours I spent at the computer and the times we weren't together because I was writing. He helped me find a comfortable desk chair with great wheels; I could send myself for a ride or a spin in the big space near the desk when I needed a break.

I think I'm learning to play. Yesterday, I did play. It was a simple card game with my granddaughter. I wasn't pretending to have fun—I did have fun. I love that. I want to experience more of that.

I feel different inside. I have found myself. I believe I am, finally, the person I was meant to be. I feel comfortable. I feel grounded and present and more confident.

I give a lot of credit to the two main methods I used for healing. Usually, therapists don't do this energy healing and energy healers don't do therapy. These methods are entirely different. To other therapists and energy healers, they don't seem compatible for a variety of reasons. I see them as complementary. What one method couldn't do, the other did.

For three years, I've been pulling out old, neglected memories from my brain and body while writing this book. Recently, I've felt compelled to pull out old, neglected items from the drawers, cupboards, and closets in my home. They have been stuffed for years, just like those memories have been stuffed in me. On the outside, the house looks tidy, like I do, but behind closed doors, both places have been in a state of embarrassing confusion. I follow the same process for my stuff as I do for my memories: I look it over and decide if I can use it. I find a few jewels. I throw away a lot.

In a little desk drawer where I keep my old passport and birth certificate, I discovered a slew of ancient Indian-head nickels, worn almost smooth. My son gave them to me to keep, temporarily when he moved across the country twenty-five years ago. He's going to be happy I found them. Now, where is the bundle of real silverware I promised to give my daughter?

I picture myself, after a break for fun, cleaning my house from top to bottom and inside everything. I'll clear out all but the necessary and desirable. I've done that with myself—doing that with my house should be easy, I think.

REFLECTIONS

I wrote the following Reflections and those at the ends of chapters when I saw the changes I was trying to bring about were happening.

SUNDAY MORNING

No church today, we decided. I spent my time this morning with incest research for this book. It's been a few years since I read anything like that. The information was thorough and extensive. Afterward, I felt heavy mentally, and physically.

The author described precisely what my incest experience was like for me— disorganization, disorientation, dissociation, intense pain. That felt so personal. How did he know? I felt fully understood by this man. How often does that happen?

My husband suggested we go out for lunch which we rarely do on a Sunday. He wanted to surprise me with our destination. We drove a half-hour to a place we had liked last summer. We live near one of the Great Lakes, and the restaurant was on the water's edge. It was perfect spring weather—warm enough, sunny, and breezy.

I tripped a little on the stone steps leading down to the patio, and we haven't even tasted the margaritas yet. I have spent too much time writing and not enough on exercise. I'm not as agile as before. The margaritas are delicious. Ordinarily, we don't drink during the day, or much in the evening, if at all.

It's a big patio and the tables are spread out. I like their loud music this time. I love the way it takes over my brain, so there's nothing else going on in there. This music is Mexican, as is the food.

Out on the lake, three sailboats are heeling against the breeze. Years ago, I sailed too. I feel nostalgic for a moment. This is one of my favorite scenes—sunshine in early summer, a magical day on the lake.

What a difference between this scene and my task this morning. That morning shadow leaves me. This is what is real now. This is my life now. I cry some, but it's happy crying. I am so grateful I'm where I am now.

A man and his daughter, I assume, from the table closest, but not too close, start a leisurely walk toward the lake. She's about four years old and cute as can be. The little girl has blond hair and wears a colorful dress. She could be a young me. The man is dressed casually. He looks like a regular guy who would have a job and a family. After a bit of exploring they stroll back. The child leads the adult now. No hurry.

He has nothing more important to do than to follow along with his little girl. Sigh. It must be nice. I acknowledge a moment of envy.

There's a beanbag toss game on the grass in front of us. The little girl tries to gather up all the bean bags in her arms. The man helps her hold onto them, and then he helps her put them back. They gradually make their way back to the table where their people are sitting.

Now, I'm really in tears. I cry when something is beautiful. I cry when I'm happy and when something touches my heart. This was a precious scene. I'm delighted for all the little girls whose daddies let them lead the way, and don't always insist on being in charge, and don't do terrible things that hurt them.

This daddy never looks toward those of us who are watching. I wonder—maybe he's a monster behind closed doors. I hope, a lot, that he's not. Abusers can look so good in front of other people.

This father/daughter scene touches my soul. I'm glad nobody can notice my tears. This morning when I was reading that incest research for my book, my old life was highlighted. In the past, I was always afraid and ready for the worst. Then the worst would happen.

But this afternoon is my present life. I can live in the moment and enjoy the riches my senses present to me, and the many joys in my life. My blessings are plentiful. I feel them. I love them. I'm doing my soul's work. I'm grateful.

LOVE

I Love more. I feel more loving. I feel and trust the love of the people who love me. As I behave more lovingly, I see them being more loving—my husband, my children, my grandchildren, my husband's family, my few friends and people I don't even know.

I love myself more. I no longer pick on, punish, blame, or berate myself. I was so harsh with myself. Now, if I regret what I realize later I could have and should have done differently, I say to myself, "Just do it this way next time."

EARLY SUCCESS

I can't believe it. I finally did it. "I cracked the case," as my co-worker psychotherapist used to say when she thought her client's problems were solved. But this time, it is my case. I finished much of it yesterday. With the Body Code, I let go of my negative program having to do with the loss of Angel. I had decided at age six to have as little contact as possible with others so I could protect myself from being hurt like that again. That decision had stuck to me like Gorilla Glue.

Ordinarily, we make these decisions at a young age in times of difficulty, out of fear, with incomplete information. Then we continue to act on them and never look back.

As I said, contact with others had been best for me in structured, limited situations. With more extended visits,

I often felt trapped and eager to get away. That was true even when I was with my grown children whom I adore. The times when I did want more contact, I couldn't change my feelings and behavior by trying to do better or wishing I were different. Now, I *am* different.

It's hard to know where I am in the healing process because I don't know what I don't know. I can think I'm finished before I am. I like to feel I have progressed and have everything under control, but then there's the next stage. I work at it again and think I'm done. Now I think I am done, because....

I'm bolder. Today I visit the little market where I have gone for twenty years to buy fresh sweet corn. I believe the man who grows and sells it is afraid of people, too, because he seems cold and doesn't talk. It takes one to know one. After twenty years, I don't have any sort of friendly relationship with him.

Usually, I try to beat him at his game, but today I greet him pleasantly. "Good morning. I would like one dozen, please. I like my corn to be young with small, crunchy kernels."

No response. We exchange the bag of corn and money. Trying again, I ask, "Did you have a good summer with your corn crop?"

He looks at me for the first time. I notice his weather-worn face. He replies, "Yes, I did. Production will last into October."

I say, "Good. Thank you."

I say to myself, "Okay. Not bad."

At the carpet store, I tell the rug guy, whom I've never seen before, "I need a replacement pad under my area rug, because our cat pooped on the rug, and while it was out being cleaned, we messed up the pad with dirty footprints and such. Then we were too scared of repeat poops to put the clean rug back on the floor soon enough, so the rug pad is dirtier than ever." I reject the idea that this self-disclosure might be a tad inappropriate and not what the man wants to hear. Today, I quickly decide it won't hurt him. This is what I want to say. I've always had that noisy voice in my head that outlawed my spontaneity.

After that lovely sharing, the rug guy tells me quite a bit about his card-playing and more about his life. Then we get to the topic of who I know that lives on his street.

Really, I have never participated in a conversation like this with a stranger, yet I am comfortable with it. I enjoy it. It feels like I've been talking to people all my life. In the past, though, I was the one who stood in the background and watched and waited impatiently while other people made friends.

While I'm driving home, the sky looks incredibly blue. Cumulus clouds blanket most of the blue parts and overlap each other, like a painting in which the painter went overboard with cloud production. My vision is clear. I may be seeing the sky for the first time. It's beautiful. I am grateful.

Earlier in the day, I felt my jaws relax again, which indicated to me that I had let go of some heavy tension and perhaps the desire to keep my mouth shut. Now my shoulders lower some inches from their usual tensed position. I can stick my neck out more now. Those body events are evidence that significant change has occurred. I feel them. I love them.

A few months later, I went to a party by myself, which is a rare and scary event, ordinarily. This time I am happy to be there. I smile at everyone—the strangers and the ones I have known for years, but not very well. All seem harmless today. I am comfortable. I wait for my usual party anxiety to show up, but it doesn't. I can talk to others; I can sit by myself without panicking.

I'm seeing people differently, and they seem to perceive me differently. They are more responsive. The changes I've made must be showing. I feel my heart turn warmer in my chest after this party. The difference in me feels monumental.

I FEEL MY HEART OPEN

I feel it happening in my chest. It's not a pain, but a feeling of pressure right in the middle of my chest which relaxes and expands my chest. Right away I know what is happening and I am delighted. I feel different about other people again. I smile at them. They smile back at me.

Everyone I encounter now seems like a real person. I had made people, except for my clients, husband, and family, not matter personally to me. Waitresses in restaurants are real people all of a sudden, instead of a necessity for getting food. How cold of me. In my effort not to be hurt again, I had de-humanized people I didn't even know. I had no idea.

I see how I made others less worthy than me or made myself less worthy than them. Something was wrong with them, or something was wrong with me, so there could never be a connection between us. I could see myself doing that over the last few years, but I was unable to change it until now.

I used to feel like I was barely allowed to belong to the human race. Now people are people, and I am just one of them. We are all the human race. They have all had their troubles, too.

The issue of trusting other people was my last big challenge and the most difficult one. My husband feels we get along better than ever because I am more trusting of him. He says I am more loving. He loves that, and in turn, is more loving toward me. I see it, too. It's remarkable the way that works.

NEW ME

I'm observing myself, as usual. What I see, at last, is me being the real me. When I talk, I hear more conviction and authority in my voice and manner. I actually speak when it's not a necessity. I talk more, but not too much. I can volunteer information about myself sometimes. It all feels good.

Yesterday, our current handyman came to fix the broken shelf and clothes-hanging system in my closet. What a mess. Two shelves had decided they wanted to be free, too, and clothes had fallen everywhere in the closet.

Typically I don't pay much attention to people who fix things in our house. I know this particular man is cranky. If you ask him a question about the work you are paying him to do, he responds as if you're attacking his integrity. I wanted to see what would happen today if I were more involved and gracious. I had the clothes out of the way and everything prepared for him. I greeted him cheerily at the door and found him the tool he said he needed but didn't bring with him. I was surprised that he was listening so well when we discussed the position of the shelves. He went to work, and I went to the gas station.

When I returned, I visited the handyman and the closet. After I admired his progress, I told him I had just tried four times to make a credit card payment for gas. I told him how our kitchen sink clogged up this morning, and all our vigorous plunging wouldn't make the water go down. He said nothing. I said nothing more.

When he finished the closet, I told him I was delighted with the results, which was true. I paid for his work, and we said goodbye. On the way out of the house, he stopped at the kitchen sink. Still saying nothing, he took the drain apart and unclogged it.

Then, he said, "God bless you," and slipped out the door.

I've heard spiritual leaders say every interaction is an opportunity to connect with another human being and spread a little good will and happiness. Now that's what I want to do more often.

CREATIVITY

I've always had creative ideas, but I was afraid to be different or stand out in any way as a child. As an adult, I still tried to do what I thought other people wanted. That killed my creativity. It's only lately that I see that being different is being myself—and being myself is being different. And it's okay. In fact, it's fun.

For years I stored an antique doll buggy that my daughter had found in the trash at her apartment building. She thought I might like it, and she was right—I loved it. But I couldn't figure out what to do with it besides planting flowers in it, and that idea didn't appeal to me. Finally, after even more years of storing this buggy, I looked at it taking up space and thought, "It's got to go." Its leather is even more worn out now and we need the storage space. What do I like about it? It's the wheels. I love the wheels. They are unique and antique. (I started to like antiques when I lived in that old house I described earlier.) I decided to take the wheels off the buggy. I hung three of the wheels on the wall in a vertical line and threw away the rest of the buggy. (I saved the fourth wheel. It was like the proverbial third wheel. Later, I gave it to my daughter-in-law to hang on her wall. I enjoyed giving it to her. It looks good at her house.) On my wall, the edges of the wheels don't touch the wall because a metal piece in the center prevents it. As a result, each wheel makes its own shadow with the spokes, which adds to the uniqueness of the wall scene. I love the wheels. I love their shadows. I had so much fun doing that.

What would other people think? If they like it, fine. If not, that's fine, too. That attitude frees me to enjoy it even more. That sounds so obvious, but it's new for me. These days, I think what other people think of me is none of my business.

I have learned so much in the healing process. I was ravenous to learn about any area of my life that was difficult, which was most of them. All my observing, learning, and putting things together helped me immensely. It has enhanced my work with others. I think I just accepted all of my past as a part of me. That allows me to be more rather than less. I feel loving toward myself and others. I feel whole.

RESULTS

I could tell my vibrations were higher due to releasing so many of the low level trapped emotions, like shame, low self-esteem, helplessness, and worthlessness. I'm aware that I smile freely and often at other people. This reminds me of that sad situation I described earlier when I couldn't smile even a fake smile, for a photo. What a difference.

When I do energy healing work with clients, I pray and thank God, silently, before I work with them. Dr. Nelson recommends that. I like it. I have expressed gratitude at every opportunity because I feel so good. Everything that has happened to me was an opportunity to grow and learn.

My friend has finally convinced me that we have angels around us to help us if we let them. I discovered a writing angel who gives me writing ideas, as well as a road angel who helps me avoid auto accidents when I'm not paying enough attention. I still try to do my part, of course. Who knows—she/he may not be paying attention, either. The universe is rewarding me over and over. It has my back.

It's lovely to feel my body's edges. My neck and shoulders have relaxed. My back lost that curve where it meets my short neck, which now looks longer. As I said before, I love these body changes. I know that real, permanent change has occurred in my psyche, as well.

CHANGES

I belong to a group, and I mean I belong to a group. I'm not the leader of the group, but I lead a mindfulness meditation at the beginning of the meetings. It's what the group wanted, and I volunteered.

Usually, when I meditate, I pay attention to my senses, thoughts, and feelings, but at a recent meeting of this group, I decided to just pay attention to my breathing. I planned to focus on breathing in and out as deeply as I could. My breathing process had roadblocks between my nose and the air's final destination for as long as I can remember. It's as if I had logs or rocks in there to trip up my breath if I tried to breathe deeply. I didn't notice it much because I'm usually a shallow breather, but for deep breathing, I would have to force the air down there. This process was unpleasant. I tried to free the passageway numerous times with lots of breathing but little success. I had given up.

This time when I started my deep breathing and took in the air, my breath just flowed in undeterred, and flowed out, undeterred. No effort at all was needed on my part. I couldn't believe it. I tried it again. It still worked. It still works now. I feel so free. Apparently, some healing intervention did the job, or I didn't need to block my feelings anymore. I'm so grateful I can breathe right. I can take a deep breath. I'm so excited.

GIFTS FROM MY PAST

When I began writing this book, I was concerned about dragging my readers through my pain and adding to theirs. In the case of incest survivors, you are already in similar pain, and that's why you are reading this book. To some of us, knowing about other survivors' pain can be affirming and encouraging. I'm not alone. Someone has been where I am and has worked through it. Maybe I can too. There is hope for me.

There is a greater emphasis in therapy, these days, on finding the positive in peoples' lives and experiences instead of dwelling so much on the negatives. I still have too much of those negative thinking tendencies, so I gave myself a task. While driving to work one morning, I tried to observe myself in the present, as if from a distance, and think from a fresh point of view. I asked myself, "If I did have some gifts from the past, what could they possibly be?" How do you find something positive in unrelenting PTSD, intense fear of other people, painful flashbacks, and a small, fear-driven life? What do I have now that I didn't have before?

Very quickly, my answer came: I enjoy challenges now, even difficult ones. I like to find solutions, and I find excellent ones. That childhood mess was a massive challenge. I not only survived, but I am doing so much better than I ever could have imagined. I am stronger, and my life is bigger.

Some tension inside my body let go at that moment. I felt bigger yet, fuller, and more grown up. Once again, I could see the past slipping away behind me and feel my soul cheering me on. I heard myself—or something—say to me, "It's okay now; it's okay." I shed a few tears. I felt whole and grounded.

If I hadn't done all that work, I would be physically, mentally and spiritually sick, without a mind of my own, dependent on others, miserable, and angry right now.

The best gift I could have is my new improved self and a greater willingness and ability to reach out and relate to others and be a part of life. The spooky thing is that without the life I had with incest and love starvation, I wouldn't have experienced the personal and spiritual growth I now enjoy.

PART TWO

CHAPTER 8

Inside Incest

In Part 2, we look at information about incest, in general, the incest family, and the incest experience. Early in my counseling career, I worked at a community counseling agency. The family incest treatment program in the community asked our agency to supply counselors who could supplement their group therapy treatment. Everyone in the treatment groups was required to have individual therapy, as well.

I agreed to meet weekly with a few individual perpetrators as well as mothers of the girls they victimized and occasionally the girls themselves, along with my regular caseload. With a more experienced therapist, I led therapy groups for mothers of the victims. I attended frequent training and coordination meetings with knowledgeable staff who taught us how to work with this population. Our training emphasized the need to hold perpetrators accountable for their behavior. This arrangement lasted for two years for me.

At the time, I was unaware of the extent and the impact of my own incest experience. Much of it was still buried. That situation could have resulted in my personal experience becoming entangled with the clients' issues. My thick layer of denial kept me from reacting to these clients personally, but I did notice how many of their family dynamics were similar to what I had experienced growing up. I was curious and apprehensive at first about working with the perpetrators. I expected them to be monsters. Instead, I discovered they were regular humans with serious problems.

The abusers in this program, all men at this time, had been charged with molestation, or more, and removed from their homes by the court system. They were screened for their potential to successfully complete this program. The record of their abuse history was sent to leaders of the groups so they could help the men be accountable for their actions. The families were monitored by Children Services.

One of the first things I learned is that incest perpetrators seek sexual gratification as the means to fulfill their need to control someone weaker. Probably, the abusers acquired this need because they, themselves, had been sexually or severely physically abused in childhood.

In general, I found these men to be self-centered and unconcerned about the effects of their behavior on the children they abused and on the girls' mothers who were their partners. As a group, they seemed numb and out of touch with themselves and the world. Perpetrators usually feel entitled to meet their own needs however they choose. When confronted by the damage caused by their behavior, they deny, defend, and excuse their actions to themselves and others. Their relationships, including sexual, with their partners, were usually unsatisfying and dysfunctional. Treatment goals for this program included having the men tell their therapy group and leader the details of what they did to the children. They needed to explain how they "groomed" and manipulated the daughter and lied to the mother. Before they completed the program, the perpetrators were required to demonstrate they understood the impact of their behavior on the victim and family. They had to be fully accountable before the court allowed them to return home.

Learning how to avoid reoffending after treatment is essential because relapses occur as they do in other kinds of recovery. Our job as counselors was to look for possible regression, ask about their behavior and support them, their treatment, and their recovery process without making the abuse acceptable in any way.

Perpetrators often require other services, such as substance abuse treatment, anger management, relationship or social skills training and psychiatric services. Personal boundaries must be learned and respected.

An example of lack of boundaries occurred in my experience with a married client who had molested both of his daughters. He asked me to go out to dinner with him after one of our afternoon counseling sessions. Although he had been taught the rules of the client/therapist relationship, he said he didn't know this invitation was inappropriate. I think he did know that he was good-looking and likable, which was rare in these groups. When I recovered from my surprise, I explained the rules again. The client said, "I didn't mean anything by it."

This situation shook me up. At the time, I didn't have the nerve to pursue the subject of boundary issues further.

Mothers of the abused daughters were seriously in need of treatment, too. Their emotional and financial dependency on the perpetrators was often a problem, as it was with my mother. Most of them knew their daughters were being molested but were in denial at the same time. Mothers often blamed their daughters for causing the abuse. They often related poorly to the girls while protecting their abusing partners. Frequently, the girls' mothers, also, had been sexually abused in childhood, and they may have been tolerating other forms of abuse from the perpetrator, such as verbal abuse or domestic violence.

The mothers of the victims needed to learn to protect and provide for their children. They needed to be prepared to stand up to the perpetrator if he was allowed by the court to return home. They must immediately report any inappropriate behavior. Or, in some cases, they needed to learn how to avoid sexually abusive men entirely.

Mothers of the victims were coached on the above, as well as how to communicate with their daughter and provide emotional support for her and what she suffered. They must stop blaming the daughter and hold the offender responsible for his behavior—past, present, and future.

The women needed to take charge, possibly for the first time. Many of these women, like my mother, were poorly equipped for the job and were hindered by their own abuse experience. In this incest family treatment program, some learned, and some didn't.

Now, I see more clearly how my family fit this pattern. Some of the abusers and mothers behaved very similarly to my parents, and the family dynamics were similar to those in my family of origin. The main difference I saw between my family and these treatment families was socioeconomic. Could a doctor receive a slap on the wrist and have the charges dropped?

In incest and other dysfunctional families, rigid rules are commonly imposed on family members. Instructions for the children and possibly the spouse are likely to include the following:

TYPICAL RULES IN INCEST, ALCOHOLIC, AND OTHER DYSFUNCTIONAL FAMILIES:

- Always be in control of yourself.
- Don't talk about your feelings.

- Don't talk about the bad things that happen.
- Don't have needs.
- Don't ask for help inside or outside the family.
- Protect the family privacy.
- Be responsible for certain family members. Excuse their bad behavior.
- *Not directly taught, but modeled*: Don't take responsibility for your own behavior.

Be defensive. Blame someone else.

In healthy families, most of the time, parents will make an appropriate, accepting response to the following normal child behavior: asking for help, expressing feelings, expressing emotional pain, acting like a child, making mistakes. Support is provided in trusting your own senses, experience, and judgment. You learn that you are not responsible for the behavior of other people, but you are responsible and accountable for your own behavior.

Healthy families support the uniqueness of each member and encourage critical thinking and asking questions while maintaining an atmosphere of trust and safety. These are goals to strive for, and no family is perfect. It must be "good enough" for the children to thrive.

Young children are innocent and vulnerable. They think they are the center of the universe. They soak up information about themselves and their world from what they see and hear in the family. They believe what their parents tell them.

Until the age of six, children cannot judge the validity of the information they receive. Children are forming a sense of self. If parents tell them they are special, beautiful, and loving, children believe that. If their parents say they are stupid, undeserving, etc., they believe that.

If they are abused and/or neglected, it is natural for young children to think they caused it. If parents or caregivers tell them the abuse was their fault, that strengthens their self-blame and adds to their pain.

If the child could put the blame on the parent(s) where it belongs, that would conflict with how the parents want to see themselves. We know, as children, that we can't survive without a parent or caregiver to take care of us, and so we have no choice but to accept their terms.

For many years, I felt I was different, and my life was different from that of other people. When I realized the reason for that, I found information about other incest survivors' experiences to be very helpful for understanding myself. It was a relief to know I was not the only one.

When I read the following article, I felt understood, validated, and informed as a survivor and a therapist. It was written by David M. Lawson, a professor in the Department of Counselor Education at Sam Houston State University and Director of the Center for Research and Clinical Training in Trauma. This article appeared in *Counseling Today* (March 2018) which is a professional publication. The purpose of the article was to provide research information to aid counselors in understanding the incest survivor's experience and needs in treatment.

Professor Lawson has given me permission to share the following information I am summarizing from his article. It's a lot to take in all at once. I include it to help my readers understand what they may be experiencing and to know that others have been where they are now. If it seems too intense at this time, feel free to skip some or all of it. Or, you might want to read it in small doses:

Perpetrators of incest can be biological, step, or foster fathers, grandfathers, uncles, cousins, siblings, or female counterparts. Incest creates high levels of secrecy, betrayal, and powerlessness in the family. It produces conflicted loyalties and the fear of punishment. Incest creates shame and self-blame in the survivor. Survivors of father-daughter incest, especially, are likely to experience feelings of low self-esteem and self-worth, self-loathing, and lack of confidence. Other prevalent feelings can be worthlessness, helplessness, and contamination.

The average length of time incest occurs in a family is four years. The severity of the survivor's symptoms depends on a variety of factors: the age the sexual abuse began, its frequency and duration, and the degree of force, coercion or intimidation involved. Parental blame and negative judgment, as well as self-blame and shame, increase the severity of the symptoms, as does the occurrence of penetration.

The earlier the incest begins and the longer it lasts, the more likely it is for the survivor to choose to avoid present and future interpersonal relationships with others. Those same factors also increase the likelihood that the victim will use dissociative responses during sexual abuse and when experiencing different kinds of stressful situations. (Dissociation is the temporary loss of present awareness.)

Early incest trauma affects a child's neurological development. It often leads to a shift from the learning brain (prefrontal cortex) to the survival brain (brain stem). Greater activation of the primitive brain occurs with the need for self-protection. Early childhood victims can develop a sense of mistrust and danger that affects their perception of relationships and the world around them.

When relating with others, when the preference would be to avoid them, the individual may experience dissociation, low frustration tolerance, and defensiveness. She may treat others in a placating manner.

Some victims experience a distorted sense of their inside and outside worlds; in extreme cases, this may result in multiple personalities.

As I previously stated, statistics show that only 30% of incest cases are reported by survivors. Research indicates 1 in 20 families with a female child has a history of father-daughter sexual abuse, while 1 in 7 blended families with a female child has experienced stepfather-stepdaughter child sexual abuse. Three percent of males who reported sexual abuse as children reported mother-son incest. Most of the incest research has focused on father-daughter incest.

"Complex trauma" involves additional types of abuse—such as physical and emotional —occurring along with sexual abuse. Or it might be repetitive experiences of fewer types of abuse. This can create different kinds of problems for the victim than a one-time rape might, for example. The problems with complex trauma show up in lack of self-organization, including disturbances in emotions, sense of self, and relationships with others.

Problems with emotions include the inability to manage feelings which can result in over-reactions, outbursts, impulsive and reckless behavior, and dissociation. Disturbances with the sense of self include feeling defeated, diminished, and worthless, accompanied by feelings of shame, guilt, and despair.

Disturbances in relationships include difficulty with feeling close to others and having little interest in relationships or social involvement. Victims with complex trauma who have casual connections may be unable to maintain them.

The lack of a consistent, coherent sense of self and one's surroundings can create a continual state of anxiety and hypervigilance with the expectation of imminent danger. These individuals with complex trauma need to establish a sense of safety and strong coping skills.

Problems occurring in the incest family are likely to include contradicting messages, conflict between parents, and inappropriate alignments between some family members against one or more other family members, all within an atmosphere of denial and secrecy.

Mothers with a history of sexual abuse may enable father/ daughter incest when they choose the abusers over their daughters. The mother abandonment may have a greater negative impact on the daughter than the sexual abuse. The rejection not only reinforces the victim's sense of worthlessness and shame but may also suggest she somehow deserves it.

Victims are more likely to receive support for their abuse from family members if the abuser is a stranger or is not living in the household. That is due to denial and loyalty issues when the perpetrator lives in the home.

Betrayal trauma and betrayal blindness are recently developed concepts that explain the effects on some survivors of trauma perpetrated by someone on whom the child depends. The victim loses conscious awareness or memory of the betrayal. Or, the abused person could justify or blame herself for causing the abuse. This is an adaptive measure for blocking that information from consciousness, so it won't affect the parent/child relationship, which is necessary for survival.

The depersonalization and derealization which some victims experience distort the individual's sense of self and her sensory input of the environment. These individuals often report that people, shapes, sizes, colors, and intensities of these perceptions can change quickly and dramatically.

Alternatively, one's environment could look dull, dreary, or distant.

Trauma bonding can occur when the survivor takes on the view of the abuser, who maintains to the victim that their relationship is affectionate and caring. This can influence the survivor to choose partners similar to the abuser who will then abuse her without her realizing it.

Studies of incest survivors indicate that having erotic experiences during early childhood sexual abuse can disrupt these individuals' adult sexuality. Those subjects in this research tended to have sexual intercourse earlier and had more sex partners. They were likely to have casual sex outside of their primary relationships. They were more likely to engage in sex for money than other survivors. They were less likely to identify their childhood abuse as adults.

Many survivors of incest can "forget" their abuse. It can surface years later when the memories are triggered by specific events, or the body and mind are no longer able to hold back the memories.

I hope the above information from Professor Lawson's article proves helpful. I know it may be difficult to read and consider.

I think one of the reasons the body/mind holds back memories of incest is to avoid the experience of shame. Shame is a powerful feeling of being a terrible person, unworthy of love or belonging. It can be the belief and/or the feeling of being hopelessly flawed and unlovable. Shame can be a single experience, or it can be experienced throughout one's life.

Shame affects our self-image and can lead to disconnection from others. It can lead to depression or other mental health issues. In contrast, guilt is about what you did, whereas shame is about who you are. Shame is closely linked to incest and other kinds of abuse. Shaming the victim often appears in families where verbal abuse is prevalent. Survivors of child sexual abuse often feel, "I don't *make* a mistake, I *am* a mistake. I don't have *low* self-esteem, I have *negative* self-esteem."

The effects of shame can be counteracted by developing compassion for yourself for what you have experienced and learning to love, forgive, and accept yourself as you are. It's important to know that everyone feels some shame and that those feelings are not reality. It's important to differentiate between who you are and what you do.

One way you can counteract shame is to go to a playground or children's event and watch children who are the same age you were when you were first abused. Look how young and vulnerable they are. Would you blame these children for abuse if they were sexually abused by an older person?

My mother, for example, actually believed if a child chooses to sit on her father's lap, she is causing him to sexually abuse her. Every day millions of children, especially little girls, sit on their fathers' laps because it is a source of love, security, connection, and safe cuddling.

Child sexual abuse is never the child's fault. If the child is inappropriate sexually, the adult's job is to say "no" and gently find out what happened. She is reacting to something that was done to her. She is "acting it out."

SIGNS OF CHILD SEXUAL ABUSE

Physical: Bladder or vaginal infections, stomach aches, changes in eating habits.

- **Emotional:** Nightmares, difficulty concentrating, afraid to be alone with a certain person. The child becomes clingy and afraid to be alone at night, shows signs of depression, anxiety, or PTSD.
- **Behavioral:** Demonstrates aggressive or violent play or acting out, shows more knowledge of sex than one would expect for the age, is unwilling to change clothes or bathe, cuts self with sharp objects to let the feelings out. The artwork shows dark colors or people left out or crossed out of pictures. The child shows other behavior, not typical of that child.

An abused child may give clues to teachers, school personnel, and parents about what is happening—possibly in a vague or disguised form. The response by adults needs to be appropriate and validating. The child needs to know she is doing the right thing by telling.

People who work with children need to be educated about what to look for and how to handle it. In many cases, they are not. Various types of medical workers, for example, may be in a position to recognize sexual abuse. The child may not tell the doctor she was abused, but she might tell the office secretary. Probably, she will tell no one.

STAYING SAFE NOW

If you have a childhood history of being abused, you are more vulnerable to further abuse. If you have been forced to give up control of your body before, you may not see abuse coming or know it when you see it. You want good-for-you experiences now.

Some men see our vulnerabilities and choose women who are easy targets. They know how to be charming and give you a little of what you want to get what they want. Some men think getting away with something with women is a game. (We lose.) Sometimes it's a competition with other men.

If he is famous or forceful or has control over your job, you are more likely, under duress, to allow him to do what you don't want. If you listen to the signals in your gut—*this guy is creepy*—and you follow your gut, you will be forewarned and better prepared to protect yourself. If you are assertive instead of angry, you may not lose your job (if he is the boss) or your friend (if he's a friend).

What to do to refuse if this person matters:
(If he doesn't matter, tell him to buzz off).

- If he's touching you, look at his eyes. Say, "No. Don't touch me that way."
- If you need to say more, say, "I don't want that kind of relationship." "I" statements about you are more effective than "you" statements about him. Say what you want or don't want. Make it about you. Make it BRIEF.
- Don't argue with him. The way to stop an argument is for you to stop talking. Don't defend your right to stand up for yourself. Of course, you have that right.
- Instead of saying something new, repeat your original statement, if necessary. Say it as many times as needed. "No. Don't touch me."
- If you are respectful to him, even though he is not respectful to you, you model the kind of behavior you want him to use with you.
- Practice in the mirror at home, when you have advance warning. Look at your eyes in the mirror and say the words above out loud. Do you look and sound forceful and firm? Practice until you look and sound forceful and firm. If you don't feel it, fake it.
- Substitute *talk* for *touch* when it's verbal abuse. "Don't talk to me that way."

IF THIS BECOMES A PHYSICAL ATTACK, RUN, AND CALL FOR HELP!

Some men, and society as a whole—including women—need to change the way they perceive and treat females. Men need to re-examine their roles and behaviors. Some need to learn that what they thought was appropriate to say or do to women is offensive. Or, if men know they are offensive, they need to learn that women will no longer tolerate such behavior.

CHAPTER 9

For the Survivor

Maybe your sexual abuse memories and feelings are showing up now, or you've been working on your trauma for years, or you are somewhere in between. Wherever you are in this process, you may wish with all your heart the abuse had never happened, and the feelings would just go away and leave you alone.

I wish this hadn't happened to you, too. It's tragic to suffer through incest in childhood. It's more tragedy to need to deal with it again later on but there's hope for you and your future.

Remember this:

- The abuse is over. That was the worst part. What you experience now are memories in various forms.

- What you may be experiencing now could be your body and brain telling you it was your fault. Childhood sexual abuse is never the child's fault.
- Sexual abuse, and whatever went with it, was not what you wanted even if it felt good sometimes. You didn't cause it. It's not okay that it happened.

However, when you can accept that it happened, life is more comfortable because you are no longer fighting with reality. It happened. It's not your fault, but it's your mess to clean up. I'm sorry about that, too.

All human beings suffer in some way. Survivors can learn and grow and become the people they want to be and were meant to be. They are likely to become more kind, strong, lively and wise.

The following information can help you manage your feelings about the abuse and plan what to do.

SELF-ASSESSMENT

Sometimes it's difficult to determine if someone's touch or behavior was sexually abusive. The person doing it was likely to deny or discount your concern. After you answer these questions, if you are still in doubt, check with a mental health professional.

Was it abuse?

- Did I want that to happen?
- Did it make me feel violated?
- If the person touched you in a private area, did it feel both pleasurable and unpleasant at the same time?
- Did the person say it was an accident? Do I believe that?
- Do I feel I okay about what happened?
- Can I let this go permanently?

For an explanation of what constitutes sexual abuse, see the Glossary at the end of this book.

Are you experiencing any of the following?

- Excessive anxiety or depression
- Suicide plans
- Difficulty eating or sleeping
- Substance abuse
- Concerns about post-traumatic stress disorder

Each of these indicates the need for outside help—at least a visit to your primary care physician. Hormonal, nutritional, or other physical imbalances can affect your mental health and cause unpleasant symptoms of anxiety or depression. Please check that out with your doctor, even if you would rather not. If you don't have a doctor, it's essential to find one and use her/him.

Adverse Childhood Experiences

Adverse experiences in childhood can interfere with your development. They can lead to harmful life outcomes, such as alcohol, drug abuse/dependency, suicide attempts, sleep disturbances, disease, and other health conditions.

Several kinds of traumatic experiences are not included in this questionnaire, such as bullying, racial discrimination or death of a family member; but the examples given might help you determine the overall level of traumatic or stressful events in your early life. A score of three or more yes answers suggests a risk for possible adverse outcomes and the need for you to take precautions.

Adverse Childhood Experience Questionnaire (ACE)

While you were growing up, during your first 18 years:

1. Did a parent or other adult in the household *often*:
   swear at you, insult you, put you down,
   or humiliate you, or act in a way that made
   you afraid you might
   be physically hurt?   Check, if Yes____

2. Did a parent or other adult in the household *often*:
   push, grab, slap, or throw something at you,
   or ever hit you so hard you had
   marks or were injured?   Yes____

4. Did you *often* feel that:
   no one in your family loved you or
   thought you were important or special,
   or your family didn't look out for each
   other, feel close to each other,
   or support each other?   Yes____

5. Did you *often* feel that:
   you didn't have enough to eat, had to
   wear dirty clothes, and had no one to
   protect you, or your parents were too
   drunk or high to take care of you, or take
   you to the doctor if you needed it?   Yes____

6. Were your parents ever separated or divorced? Yes____

7. Was your mother or stepmother:
   often pushed, grabbed, slapped, or had
   something thrown at her, or *sometimes*
   or often kicked, bitten, hit with a fist, or hit
   with something hard, or *ever* repeatedly
   hit at least a few minutes or threatened
   with a gun or knife?   Yes____

8. Did you live with anyone who was a
   problem drinker or alcoholic or who
   used street drugs?   Yes____

9. Was a household member depressed or
   mentally ill, or did a household member
   attempt suicide?   Yes____

10. Did a household member go to prison?   Yes____

Add up your "Yes" answers: ____

This is your ACE Score. A score of three or more yes answers suggests a risk for possible adverse outcomes.

SOOTHING AND COPING SKILLS

Grounding Technique

This can be helpful if you are dissociating or having a flashback, or if you think you might be. If you are just feeling disconnected from yourself, grounding is a way to reconnect with yourself, in the present – with what is actually happening right now.

Look around you. Notice the details and name what you see in your current surroundings. Remind yourself where you are. Recall today's date to reorient yourself to the present. Feel your feet touching the ground. Feel the earth's energy coming up through your legs. If it's possible, it's more effective to stand outside on the dirt in bare feet for this. Recite the alphabet backward to connect with your thinking brain.

If you are already doing yoga or meditation, either could help calm your nervous system.

For Emotional Pain

Give yourself plenty of compassion. Many of us didn't receive compassion as children. Even if you can give it to others, you may need to learn to give it to yourself. It will feel good when you can do it. It requires some allowing and accepting of your painful feelings.

In my thesaurus, some synonyms for compassion are: empathy, feeling, commiseration, concern, kindness. The opposites of compassion are interesting, too: indifference, cold-bloodedness, disregard. That's what you don't want to give yourself. Compassion works. You do deserve it, even if you don't think so.

If you have difficulty being kind to yourself, think of how you would feel if your good friend described your incest experience as her/his own. What would you feel for your friend? What would you tell her to help her feel better?

When you are trying to make a decision for your life, ask yourself, "What would a person who loves herself/himself do?"

What to do When You Feel Desperate

Make a list such as the following when you feel good:

- Pet the dog/cat.
- Listen to music.
- Call someone.
- Listen to guided imagery or relaxation material to help you relax.
- Take a fast (or slow) walk.
- Enjoy nature.
- Recognize that grieving is necessary with any kind of loss, no matter how long ago your abuse occurred.

Seek Support

- Caring friends, family members, professionals.
- Hobbies, skills, and other interests.
- Spiritual support.
- A group of like-minded people.

Your Feelings Are Your Friends

Under normal circumstances, feelings can give you essential information about yourself. When they are overwhelming, they can push you to extremes, or they can shut down. If you follow these soothing practices, you may be able to help them calm down, instead of shut down. See if you can name your feelings and acknowledge their presence.

Watch Your Thinking

Grieving about what happened to you is necessary for healing. Sometimes it's important to distract yourself, so your mind doesn't crank out endless worry. Beating yourself up for what you did or didn't do is not necessary or helpful. Take a break. Tell those negative, critical thoughts, "no."

Survivors tend to dwell on the belief that they should have done something to stop the abuse. Our nervous system's available responses to trauma are fight, flight, and freeze. Freeze often occurs automatically; it's the life-saving response your body decides you need. (Some wild animals do that, too).

Another troubling thought is, "It shouldn't have felt good." The human body was created to respond to sexual stimulation in spite of conflicting emotions. Unwanted or inappropriate sex can still be sexually stimulating. That doesn't mean you wanted it, caused it, or asked for it, or that it's your fault.

Think about what is good in your life now. Be grateful for what you find.

Deep Abdominal Breathing

1. Place one hand on your abdomen.
2. Exhale fully through your nose or mouth. Feel your abdominal muscles contract as you push out the air.

3. Inhale through your nose and send the air into the bottom of your lungs. Your hand will rise. Your chest moves only slightly; shoulders remain still.
4. Exhale slowly and fully. Allow your body to let go of the tension.
5. Pause for a moment between each inhalation and exhalation, then repeat. Breathe slowly and regularly. Your breathing will slow as you relax. If you are stressed, increase the length of the exhalation.

Relaxation Techniques

- **Body Scan**—a gentle relaxation method. Start at your toes and slowly work your way up to the top of your head. Notice areas of tension. Release them and then move on.
- **Progressive Muscle Relaxation**—a more active relaxation method. To identify and relax specific areas of tension in your body, start at your toes. Tighten each area and then relax the muscles there before you move on.

Mindfulness Meditation

This works well for many people with a wide variety of problems. It can calm your nervous system and lower your stress. However, if you try it a few times and find that it makes you feel more upset rather than less, you may need to learn to accept your stressful feelings first. Start to allow those feelings to be there. Start to accept them.

Mindfulness meditation is paying attention in the present moment to whatever shows up in your thoughts, feelings, senses, and body sensations without your judging any of it. You notice what you experience, and let it go.

Sit comfortably in a chair with good posture and your feet flat on the floor. Close your eyes, if that's comfortable for you. Breathe deeply.

As you attempt to focus on what you are experiencing in the present moment, your mind will wander to the future or the past. When you notice that, just bring your attention back to your breathing and your present awareness. Whatever comes up for you, be with it for a moment, accept it, and let it go.

These are the benefits: Mindfulness meditation works for relieving stress, anxiety, depression, and addictive behavior. You can train yourself to pay attention and to change your mood by focusing on the present instead of re-hashing the past or catastrophizing about the future. You can learn to be compassionate to yourself because you don't judge yourself. You are being with yourself, as you are. This can be soothing and beneficial.

Yoga

Yoga is relaxing to your body, brain, and nervous system, and over time, can make positive changes that go beyond relaxation. You will learn proper breathing, some meditation, being present in the moment, body awareness, and tolerance of bodily feelings. Yoga improves body function. It reduces anxiety and depression.

Comforting Your Inner Child (Children)

When you feel sad, anxious, depressed, scared, etc. find a doll, a stuffed animal or a pillow to represent your inner child. Hold it or place it next to you. Pay attention to how you are feeling right now. That is what your inner child is feeling. Now, you are the adult. Talk to her about what she feels, which is really what you feel right now. "I know you feel sad, (mad, lonely,)" etc. I'm sorry you feel that way. I'm here for you. I love you. I will take care of you."

Tell your inner child what would sound good to you to hear right now. "You are a wonderful person. I love you a lot. I'm sorry you are struggling," etc. If your inner child wants to talk to you, listen with love. This is a way of giving yourself what you needed as a child and what you need now. It's never too late.

When you recover from feeling foolish, and have some practice being compassionate toward yourself, this activity can feel soothing and healing. If this practice resonates with you, it will be a useful tool. If not, try returning to it later.

There is a different version of inner child work available that is gaining acceptance in the therapy community and is taught and used by therapists. See that in the therapy section, *Different Kinds of Healing Work.*

Screaming in the Car

Seriously, with closed windows. Screaming or making loud noises can relieve pent-up feelings of anger, frustration, tension, etc. When I first tried this, I could barely make a squeak. I am really loud now. I consider this an accomplishment. It feels like I'm letting go of something when I scream as loud as I can. (I check to be sure no cars or pedestrians are around me, and I'm careful not to damage my throat.) Sometimes I scream words; sometimes, I scream aaaahhhhh. It feels good. Frequently, now, they are happy screams, and I'm expressing positive energy—as if my team has made a touchdown.

12-Step Groups

These include AA, Alanon, Overeaters's Anonymous, Sex and Love Addicts Anonymous, NA (Narcotics Anonymous). You can find them online. You can attend meetings of AA and Alanon near where you live. They can be helpful and supportive. Alanon is for codependents; AA if you have a drinking/drug problem. Treatment for drinking/drug dependency may be needed, also. Seeking treatment for trauma and addiction together is a good option many survivors.

Some sex abuse survivors have difficulty with the AA concept of powerlessness over your addiction. They feel they have already experienced enough powerlessness over their lives because of their sexual abuse. However, be aware that the way the word is used in AA is different. Perhaps you can find a substitute word or come to see the meaning of the word differently.

Gratitude

Practice being grateful for what you have. The worse you feel, the more essential it is to find what you can be thankful for. For example, can you breathe, walk, and talk? If you establish a practice of naming what you are grateful for, it will make you feel better when you do it. I use this practice when I am driving my car. It is automatic (the car and the practice). I also consciously practice gratitude when I appreciate something beautiful or special that happens in my world.

Journaling and Writing Letters You Don't Send

Journaling can help you organize your thoughts and gain insight into what you feel and think. It can help you release your feelings. You can do it daily or just when you feel like it. A regular journaling practice shows you the progress and changes you have made, as well as the issues you need to work on. It can help you clarify your values and your sense of self. Don't try to make it good writing. Use stream-of-consciousness writing where you simply let your thoughts flow and write them down.

Writing a letter you don't send can be a powerful way of expressing your pain and anger. You can write anything you want. You can be mean—it's just for you. This writing can be helpful and painful and relieving, all at once. When you finish it, you might feel like sending it to the perpetrator. I wouldn't advise it. You won't be able to see the reaction or hear what you might want to hear. You may lose an opportunity in the future for a face to face meeting and a response from the abuser. Instead, tear it up.

TREATMENT OR NO TREATMENT?

The kind and amount of treatment you might need depends on the severity of your trauma and how much it affects you. You may not know the long-term effects yet. The severity ranges from a single molestation to years of complex trauma. You could talk about your situation with a therapist to help you decide how to proceed. Although you probably want to get over this experience as quickly as possible because it's painful, minimizing it or trying to ignore it may not be the best plan.

In the movie, *She's Funny That Way*,[6] Isabella (who has a different kind of problem) says, "If you don't let go of your past, it will strangle your future." I believe this statement applies directly to childhood abuse.

Let's say that no treatment could be a valid choice for some people. You can get on with your life. You can focus on what you want, need, and love to do. You can focus on your relationships. You can ignore the pain rather than stir it up—if that works. You can save time and money... but please keep reading.

Without psychological help, you may not feel as good as you would after some treatment. The trauma stays with you. Other people, movies, or TV programs could trigger your trauma feelings. It may become more intense later in life.

Consider this: If you have children now or will have them in the future, you could easily pass the effects of your trauma down to your children. A moderate amount of therapy would help you to explore and make sense of your past. You need to know what was passed down to you so you can avoid passing it down to your children.

Without treatment, you may know something about child abuse in general, but you won't know what applies to you. You may not respond appropriately if your child tells you someone is abusing her. The difficult feelings you can't see in yourself, you will see in others. If you remain hurt, you will likely hurt others—friends, spouse, etc.

People who think you should just "get over it" don't understand. No matter how long ago the events happened, trauma can be re-experienced throughout your life in some sort of disguise. Our feelings can only be experienced in the present. Because of that, when you feel the childhood pain that remains with you from the past, you can only experience it in the present moment. It can quickly become mixed up with the actual here and now and the people in your current life.

I have noticed that many survivors (including me, until I dealt with my abuse) can be overly annoyed at someone in their current life—such as a child, husband or boss, for example—and under-annoyed at their abuser or those who enabled the abuser. In other words, we can sometimes, unknowingly, make the current people in our lives responsible for upsetting us in the present, instead of attributing the feelings we have to the abuser way back in the past where the feelings originate. Unconsciously, we avoid that because it would bring us in contact with the pain we are trying not to feel.

This creates a real problem for the person on the receiving end. I was on the receiving end with my mother. She made me responsible for the pain that stemmed from her own childhood sexual abuse and neglect. I took the brunt of it when she re-lived it.

Our resistance to pain can be worse than the pain itself. We want to hide from the fear and the feelings of emptiness.

Instead of using alcohol, food, sex, etc., to avoid the discomfort, if we stay present we can learn to tolerate the feelings. We can even meet those feelings with kindness, openness and compassion with ourselves. That takes some practice. You are in charge now.

An essential goal for moderate treatment is to look at what happened enough so that you can make meaning out of it when it comes up again. That will happen at different life stages and events. Your grief, anger, shame, etc., will show up in disturbances with sex, marriage, or childbirth, for example, or when your child becomes the age you were, when you were first abused.

Without treatment, your relationship with yourself and others could suffer. Your ability to love and relate to friends and lovers could be damaged because of unhealed trauma. It's scary to be intimate if you have unresolved pain from sexual abuse or the emotional neglect that usually accompanies incest. Sex will be less satisfying to you and your partner. Trauma doesn't have to define you, but it could if you try to avoid it.

In the process of exploring your options, if you decide to deal with the effects of the trauma, you will need to gradually face your feelings and body sensations. With a moderate amount of therapy, you can get your life under enough control to be able to live with what's left and seek treatment when it bothers you. You may write a narrative which describes your life in a more positive light. Many survivors manage their trauma this way.

If you want to go all the way to inner freedom, you work at healing until you feel finished and you feel excellent. You love yourself and other people. You have clear knowledge of what happened to you, how it affected you, and what you need to attend to as a result of the trauma. You find your real self and make your life the best it can be. The work is part of your life. The rewards can be significant.

The overall goal of trauma treatment is to become resilient. You can cope with difficulties and recover from stress, regulate your emotions, view adversity in a more positive light, give and receive emotional support with others, and take care of yourself. You can give and receive love and enjoy sex.

IDEAS FOR PERSONAL GOALS FOR HEALING

- Create or re-create your sense of personal power.
- Reduce shame and negativity.
- Create appropriate boundaries.
- Stop or reduce the use of substances to numb the pain.

IDEAS FOR THERAPEUTIC GOALS FOR HEALING

- Maintain safety.

- Develop or increase self-regulation of feelings, thoughts, behavior, relationship with others and yourself.
- Develop coping skills.

POSSIBLE ADDITIONAL THERAPEUTIC GOALS

- Resolve and integrate traumatic memories by processing them, making meaning of them, and mourning losses.
- Construct a self-narrative.
- Enhance feelings of self-worth and self-esteem through the cultivation of personal creativity, imagination, achievement, mastery, and the capacity to experience pleasure.
- Develop interpersonal skills such as assertiveness, cooperation, boundary and limit-setting, social reciprocity, social empathy and the capacity for physical and emotional intimacy.

HOW I APPROACH MY HEALING WORK

"Awareness is curative." This means that if you can become fully aware of what happens with you regarding a particular problem, you can eliminate it. It is a Gestalt therapy concept, and you can do this without a Gestalt therapist. This is a form of mindfulness.

To understand or change something about yourself, watch for the problem. Then, when you observe the problem happening, do the following:

- Stand back and observe yourself being yourself. (At first, it feels strange—as if there are two of you.)
- Pay attention to your thoughts and feelings.
- Notice your behavior.
- Be curious about yourself and how you operate.
- Develop a neutral attitude about what you observe. Don't judge yourself.
- Notice what seems odd or doesn't fit in your feelings, thoughts, behavior.
- Notice patterns. When _____ happens, I do _____.
- Notice what you don't like about yourself that relates to this problem.

Again, don't judge yourself. If you do, you will get bogged down with being critical. The process won't work, and you will quit because your self-criticism hurts. Be curious rather than judgmental. You may need practice in being compassionate toward yourself. Mindfulness meditation will help with that.

Accept what you observe. You must accept that you have the problem, or that you do the particular behavior before you can change it. A problem will not change unless you first accept that you have it. (Strange, but true).

For example, you can say to yourself, "I have this problem of losing my temper. This is where I am now. It's not going to be permanent. I'm working to change it." Then you watch yourself doing it, or acknowledge it after you do it.

Writing down your observations will keep you in touch with your work and help you notice progress.

DIFFERENT KINDS OF HEALING WORK:
Find your path; reclaim your life.

Psychotherapy or Counseling

In general, people go to therapy reluctantly, when their efforts to cope with anxiety, depression, or other difficulties have been unsuccessful, and their symptoms interfere with their daily lives. People often feel they should be able to fix their problems themselves and are ashamed to need or ask for help. Yet even therapists seek help from other therapists at times. The feeling that "nothing will help" can be a sign of depression. Some physical symptoms, such as frequent headaches, digestive issues, or fatigue, may indicate a need for therapy. Have a medical exam to rule out any physical problems which could cause mental health symptoms. Hormone and other imbalances can cause depression or anxiety.

Therapy helps you take a step back and discover new ways to view yourself and your world. (Counseling is usually brief and less in-depth.) It helps you look at and sort out your thoughts, feelings, and behaviors. The therapist serves as a guide while you do the work. In the therapy process, you will not lose anything you would want to keep, such as your individuality or creativity. With therapy, you can become more of who you are. The therapist helps you increase your awareness of your strengths. Your job is to look inside yourself, share what you can, keep your appointments, pay your fee, and do your homework if you have it.

If you go to therapy, you can find a trustworthy person to listen to you and respond appropriately. First, find out if your potential therapist has experience and interest in working with sexual abuse/incest survivors. Some do; some don't. Proceed only when he/she says yes with enthusiasm. Ask questions about training and experience. That is your right as the consumer.

Even though it's challenging to do, it can be beneficial to share your abuse experience with a trained person. The therapist won't judge you, tell you what to do (ordinarily), get tired of hearing your sad story, or tell other people what you said unless required by law. She/he will offer you hope and help.

Research shows that most healing in therapy is due not to the specific methods the therapist uses but to the relationship between you. When you feel heard and understood and have a working relationship regarding your issues, it feels like a good fit. After you get acquainted, you need to feel like your therapist "gets" you. You help him or her "get you" by saying what you are thinking and feeling. That includes what you are looking for in therapy, and in a therapist. If you have previous experience with therapy, describe what you learned from that about what you do or don't want.

If your therapist seems to belittle or scold you or to be using you to listen to his or her personal problems, find a different therapist. If you feel uncomfortable with the person or your gut tells you something is wrong, pay close attention. Any sort of personal or sexual relationship between you is inappropriate. It will hurt you in the long run and is illegal for the therapist.

Except for the above conditions, if something is not working, talk about it and see what he/she has to say. Don't drop out before trying to make the relationship work, if there's a chance it could.

Most therapists do good work, care about their clients, and are trustworthy. Working on sexual abuse issues can be uncomfortable. Trusting the therapist and being able to work together with that person is particularly important. It may be appropriate, up to a point, to shop around to find a therapist who is a good fit.

Who are the therapists? Psychiatrists are medical doctors who mostly prescribe medication. Some do therapy. Licensed counselors and social workers have master's degrees and are equally capable. Psychologists have additional education.

To find a therapist: check with your insurance company, if you have insurance, for names of covered therapists. Ask your primary care doctor or your friends and family for suggestions. Most therapists have websites you can Google. Visit therapy finder websites, such as Psychology Today's "Find a Therapist." (That site covers the U.S. and Canada.)

TYPES OF THERAPY

Although the relationship with the therapist is the most important healing tool, you also need to feel comfortable with the therapist's methods. The following therapies are appropriate for sex abuse survivors. Some therapists will see you online.

Psychodynamic Therapy

The focus is on what is currently going on inside you and getting to the root of your problems by discovering how past experiences, patterns, and forces are affecting you now. If you get to know why you do what you do, you may not need to continue what isn't helpful.

Cognitive Behavioral Therapy

The focus is on how you create your own reality and make meaning of your life through your thoughts, beliefs, and assumptions. The goal of therapy is to challenge what you assume to be true and take for granted that may not be beneficial. If this therapy is not combined with other methods, it might be too highly structured to be helpful for sex abuse survivors who want to tell their story. Ask your potential therapist about this.

I read about a time-limited (12-16 sessions) TF-CBT treatment for children who have experienced trauma. In this program, psychoeducation teaches coping and other necessary skills, such as how to identify and regulate emotions. It ends with the child writing a narrative and receiving praise for having told her story. You may be able to find an adult version of that.

Gestalt Therapy

The emphasis is on gaining insight into how you do what you do, not why. This is accomplished by focusing on the immediate experience of your senses. The goal is to integrate the disowned parts of yourself, to develop self-acceptance and live more spontaneously in the present moment. "Experiential" exercises are sometimes used in individual and group therapy.

Humanistic and Existential

Human beings are basically good. We have the freedom to choose all our actions and behaviors. No matter what our life experiences bring us, we are fully responsible for how we handle them. Emphasis is on personal responsibility.

Group Therapy for Sexual Abuse

Sharing about yourself and giving and receiving support and appropriate feedback can be invaluable to a survivor. Learning what happened to others and how they cope is helpful and reassuring. You may want to start with individual therapy, first, to get comfortable with talking about your abuse.

Sex Therapy

Some therapists specialize in helping individuals and couples with sexual issues in therapy. Others do it as part of the sexual abuse treatment. You can visit therapist websites or call them.

Attachment-Focused Therapy

Adults who were sexually abused and/or neglected as children can have issues stemming from the poor quality of the caregiving they received in early childhood. Infants need the caretaker to be sensitive to and connected with them. Without that healthy connection, dysfunctional attachment styles emerge. Depending on caretaker behavior, the unhealthy attachment style may manifest as insecure, avoidant, ambivalent, or disorganized. This therapy encourages repair of that connection and the establishment of current healthy attachment relationships, promoting healing and the ability to trust others.

Dialectical Behavioral Training (DBT)

This treatment uses a variety of cognitive and behavioral strategies with an emphasis on dialectics—the reconciliation of opposites. An example of that is accepting people as they are, versus trying to get them to change. Cognitive and behavioral therapy strategies are taught with an emphasis on skills such as mindfulness, interpersonal effectiveness, emotional regulation, distress tolerance, and self-management skills.

Eclectic

This approach is used by the majority of therapists. It tends to view people from the psychodynamic perspective while using active approaches like cognitive behavioral therapy for resolving current issues. After listening and coming to understand your issues, the therapist chooses a treatment method with your needs and preferences in mind.

OTHER TREATMENT METHODS

Eye Movement Desensitization Retraining (EMDR)

EMDR aims to neutralize and release trauma. The method, although it seems peculiar, is generally effective. After an assessment has defined and explored an issue to work on, the practitioner rapidly moves her finger back and forth while you follow it with your eyes. This is what integrates the memory in the body. It requires a practitioner trained in EMDR who is often a therapist as well. It's usually a good idea to begin with some therapy first.

Emotion Code/Body Code

This is the energy healing system I used with myself and clients, along with therapy. You can hire a practitioner and work by phone, email, Skype, in-person, or you can learn to do this work yourself. That requires first buying the program, watching the DVDs and passing the tests. The Emotion Code covers mental and spiritual issues, while The Body Code contains the Emotion Code plus everything for working with the body. See the website to learn about this work: www.healerslibrary.com and drbradleynelson.com.

Brain Theory

With the discovery that our brains can grow and change throughout our lifetimes, various methods of rewiring the brain have evolved. Books and videos on the subject of brain plasticity can teach you how to alter your thinking, eliminate habitual negative thinking, and reprogram your brain to view yourself and your world in a better light.

Dual-Diagnosis treatment

This can be a comprehensive treatment for sexual abuse trauma and addiction to drugs, alcohol, food, gambling, work, etc. if you are addicted. Have an assessment by a professional to determine if appropriate for you.

Emotional Freedom Technique (EFT) or "Tapping"

This is an inexpensive method of treatment which you can do for yourself. You can learn it online and read *the Tapping Solution* by Nick Ortner.[7] For several years the Ortner family has presented an excellent online World Summit on Tapping at the beginning of the year which provides information, demonstrations, and tap-along sessions with experts in the field. EFT is gaining some acceptance by the mainstream medical establishment. For extensive work, you may need to find an expert to guide you. It works well for trauma. It's fun to do and you get immediate results. *It costs little to learn.*

Reiki

In this hands-on energy healing method, the practitioner transfers her energy through her hands to your body where your energy is stuck. This is effective, non-threatening touch.

Inner Child

When we experience trauma, to continue to function we often abandon that traumatized part of ourselves—our inner child—which holds the pain. Then we cut it off from our awareness. That part needs to be integrated with the rest of the self to heal it. You may be able to find guidance for this from a therapist or some of the books written on the subject.

Internal Family Systems Therapy is a process that is slightly similar to inner child work. There are parts of the self which are wounded and parts that are protective to the self. With the help of the therapist, these parts can learn to work together for healing.

Trauma treatment and bodywork

The field of trauma treatment is growing, with many possible approaches now available. You have the right to ask your potential therapist about his/ her training and experience with trauma. Assess his/ her dedication to working with these clients.

Yoga

Some people view this as an actual trauma treatment method. Yoga helps to regulate the autonomic nervous system, improve breathing, and achieve better sleep and health.

Over time, yoga can help release the trauma that is trapped in the body.

Coaching

This method of helping is gaining in popularity. There are no controls over the amount of knowledge or training of the individual coach, and their instruction is brief.

YOU CAN DO IT

Healing from childhood sexual abuse is not
for the faint of heart.
If you choose it, you have to want it. You have
to do your part.
They weren't kidding when they called it *The
Courage to Heal*.[8]
Getting triggered is part of the healing deal.

Those events tell you what you need to do
To get back was taken from you.
Count your blessings if this problem is not on
your radar.
Count your blessings if it is.

You can be the best you can be,
And the person our Creator made and wanted
to see.

Healing takes time—don't forget to have fun.
You'll feel free when you are nearly done.

RESOURCES

Hotlines:
RAINN (Rape, Abuse, and Incest National Network)
800-656-HOPE
www.rainn.org

Childhelp National Child Abuse Hotline (Includes resources for adults).
800-4-a-CHILD (800-422-4453)
www.childhelp.org

National Domestic Violence Hotline
800-799-SAFE, 800-799-7233
www.ndvh.org

National Suicide Prevention Lifeline
800-273-TALK (8255)
www.suicidepreventionlifeline.org
Love Is Respect National Teen Dating Abuse Helpline
866-331-9474
www.loveisrespect.org

Books:

Each has multiple pages of resources for survivors

The Courage to Heal by Ellen Bass and Laura Davis

The Courage to Heal Workbook by Laura Davis

To contact the author:

email: madelineagarner@gmail.com

website: madelinegarner.com

EPILOGUE

Today, I'm sitting comfortably in the corner at the end of my long living room. I'm writing at the same built-in desk-bookcase-file cabinet affair that was here twenty-three years ago when I moved in. The house, which is attractive but small by today's standards, is situated in a peaceful country setting. It's only a short drive to a large city in the Midwest.

My dear second husband and our two precious cats live here, too. Our children are grown up and living elsewhere.

The girl cat is a brown and black medium-size rescue cat with a sweet, cautious disposition. Now, she is pushing her nose hard against my hand on the computer mouse. She's urging me to pet her. I love the feeling of her warm, soft fur against my hand and her "smile" of appreciation when I do it. At the same time, she's interrupting my progress. I'm impatient to get on with my writing. I'm almost finished.

Fortunately, our cats show up at our computer one at a time. The big, ginger-colored male who is sensitive, affectionate and thinks he's the lion king, likes to curl up in small boxes and tiny cat beds. Legs and other parts stick up and hang over the edges—it's so cute. At my computer, he sits on top of the printer. When we needed to buy a new printer, we could only consider the ones which were flat and sturdy on top.

A Feng Shui expert, in a book I read twenty years ago, said not to place your desk across a corner. But if you have no other choice, you will feel safer, subconsciously, if you hang a mirror in front of you at eye level. That way, you can see who might be coming toward you from behind. I had always felt "cornered" when I sat here, so when I decided to write this book, I followed his suggestion. Have you ever tried hanging a mirror in a corner?

I do feel safer now, which is important to me, as you know. The area seems more spacious with the addition of the mirror. At first, I was surprised to look up and see my face because that was not the reason for the mirror. The mirror moves a bit with the air currents, so sometimes when I look up, I'm there, and sometimes I'm not. No comment. I've finished analyzing for now.

In the morning, I welcome the reflection on the mirror of the light which floods into the window across the room behind me. Sometimes I can see a flash of red in our backyard flower garden.

Except for the mirror addition, this office set-up hasn't changed a bit in twenty years—but I have. My long struggle is over. I feel safe, happy, and comfortable. I have found myself at last. I feel transformed. I'm not perfect, and that's fine.

With this book, I send my love to you early childhood sexual abuse, emotional neglect, etc. survivors. I include, too, the people who love and work with you. Bless you, all.

Madeline

NOTES

1   P.D. Eastman, *Are You My Mother?* (Random House, Inc., 1960)
2   *The Help.* Dir.Tate Taylor. Walt Disney Studios, 2011.
3   Eckhart Tolle, *The Power of Now,* New World Library, CA, 1999
4   Dr. Bradley Nelson, The Body Code System, 2.0, Wellness Unmasked, 2009 (www.drbradleynelson.com; www.healers library.com)
5   Louise Hay, *You Can Heal Your Body,* Hay House, revised edition, 1/28/84
6   *She's Funny That Way.* Dir. Peter Bogdanovich. Lionsgate Premiere, 2014.
7   Nick Ortner, *The Tapping Solution,* Hay House, 2013
8   Ellen Bass & Laura Davis, *The Courage to Heal,* Harper, 4th edition, 2008

GLOSSARY

Anyone Can Be An Abuser: Doctor, lawyer, senator, priest, sibling, relative, female, babysitter, a younger child or anyone in a position to be near children.

Addiction to a person: Usually, one person is addicted to a substance or a behavior, and the other person is addicted to the first person. It feels as if you can't get enough of that person, you need more and more of him to fill your unmet emotional needs, and he is the main focus in your life. You are willing to put up with unacceptable behavior to get your needs met. Addiction to a person is also known as codependency.

Alanon: A support organization for codependents, focusing on how to survive and thrive even while living with an alcoholic.

Alcoholics Anonymous: A support organization for those with out-of-control drinking and/or drug use.

Alcoholism: In families, one member's addiction affects everyone in the family. This is an important issue to study if someone in your childhood was addicted.

Blaming the Victim: Assuming or claiming the victim caused the event rather than acknowledging that the abuser is responsible for his or her actions. This frequently shows up in conversations about rape. "She asked for it, she was wearing the wrong clothing, she was drunk, she shouldn't have...." That needs to be changed to, "He shouldn't have."

Codependency: Making other people more important than you are. Focusing on others and trying to fulfill their needs, trying to please them even if it is hurtful to you. Trying to fix other people so they will be what you think they should be.

Communication: Usually poor in dysfunctional families. Family rules of *don't talk* and *don't tell* develop, and communication skills are not known or taught. There is a lack of mutual sharing. Family members feel too vulnerable or fear a negative reaction if they tell each other how they feel and what hurts them, or if they ask for change. Instead, they act out or stifle their feelings. They may share and have secrets with certain family members.

Compassion: Sympathy and concern for the suffering and misfortune of others. For oneself, it is kindly acknowledging and accepting, without judgment, one's own perceived inadequacy, failure or discomfort.

Denial: A coping mechanism. Refusing to believe or accept what is real in spite of obvious evidence.

Dissociation: In your own little world, unaware and disconnected. DSM-5 Diagnostic and Statistical Manual of Mental Disorders defines dissociation as "a disruption of and/or discontinuity in the normal integration of consciousness, memory, identity, perception, body representation, motor control, and behavior."

Dysfunctional Family: Inappropriate behaviors or teachings inside the family which are designed to help the family function or solve problems. In a well-functioning family, parents are in charge, and children are heard and respected, but don't make the decisions. The parents have a close relationship with each other rather than with a child and have appropriate and loving relationships with each child. Every family has some dysfunction in it. No family is perfectly functional.

Defense Mechanisms: Used to block out the pain of reality. These include:
  Denial: It's not really happening.
  Repression: It never happened.
  Minimization: It happened, but only a little.
  Dissociation: I don't remember what happened.
  Projection: It happened to you, not me.

Elephant in the Living Room: Refers to what is being ignored in the family. Something that is big and obvious, but no one talks about it. It is incest, addiction, someone's affair, an idea or a practice that everyone believes in but nobody mentions. It could be a house overrun with clutter that someone does not "see."

Emotional Abuse: Manipulating, undermining, controlling, and taking advantage of age, strength, or other differences.

Emotional Neglect: Withholding love, appreciation, attention, support, and compassion from someone who is dependent on that person.

Empathy: Identifying with or experiencing the feelings, thoughts or attitudes of another person.

Enabling: One family member "helps" another family member do addictive or dysfunctional behavior. For example, the non-alcoholic family member buys alcohol for the alcoholic. The enabler usually does not intend to do that behavior and may not be aware of the damage involved in doing it.

Family Roles: In dysfunctional families, each member has a role. These include:

- The Mascot makes the family laugh and breaks the tension
- The Lost Child doesn't ask for anything stays in her room, isn't noticed

- The Hero makes the family look good—is good at sports, academics, etc.
- The Scapegoat who takes the blame
- Also, the Problem Person and the Chief Enabler for Problem Person

Sometimes members play more than one role.

Family Rules: Examples are: Don't talk about the family or the people in it. Don't tell the family business or secrets to anyone else. Don't feel your feelings or talk about them.

Family Secrets: Events, behavior, and feelings that would cause shame if known outside the family. For example, in my family, these included incest, my father's infidelity, my mother's mental illness, my mother's feelings about me. Those secrets often hurt the people they were meant to protect.

Fight/flight/freeze: Our nervous system's choices for a physical/emotional response to an actual or perceived life-threatening attack. When fighting or fleeing are impossible— as for an abused child—freezing is the body's natural response to the threat.

Flashbacks: Memory fragments of previous trauma showing up in the present, in dreams, nightmares, thoughts or feelings. Flashbacks can be sounds, pictures, body memories or body sensations. They can be feelings of being frozen, suffocated, trapped or taken advantage of. They are experienced in the present because feelings can only be experienced in the present.

Incest: Sexual abuse of a child by a relative or close family friend.

Inner child: An emotional part of a person that didn't grow up due to trauma.

Jekyll and Hyde: Mood swings of an alcoholic.

Minimization: One of the defense mechanisms. You recognize the problem, but you pretend that it is smaller or less important than it is.

Passive Aggressive: Behavior that is disguised resistance. You don't complain outright, you just don't do the job. You don't want to go, so you are late.

"Perfect Family" Roles: Attempt in a dysfunctional family to make the family look good to the family members and to the outside world. Having a perfectly tidy house, physical appearance, manners, etc.

Projection: If we don't like something about ourselves, and we don't want to heal it or feel it, we can attribute it to another individual or group of people. For example, I thought other people created the trouble between us, not me.

Reiki energy treatments: An effective hands-on energy healing method in which the practitioner transfers his/her energy to the client to stimulate or move the client's energy.

Repression: Memory is present but held back, unavailable because it is painful.

Role reversal: The adult plays the child's role, which forces the child to play the adult role and assume more responsibility than would be appropriate for the age of the child. For example, the child comforts the adult about adult spousal issues or does most of the housework.

Scapegoat: One of the family roles in dysfunctional families. The scapegoat is the member who is blamed, scolded, punished for what is wrong in the family.

Self-fulfilling Prophecy: When children are young and impressionable, important people in their lives define and shape them. If the statements are negative and there is little counteracting praise and encouragement, the child is likely to believe the worst about herself. She may forget she heard the words, but they can show up in her thoughts, behavior, and self-concept.

Sexual Abuse, Molestation: Forced or coerced, or held against your will by an adult or older child for someone's sexual gratification. Forced or coerced to watch sexual acts or listen to sexual talk. Sexually touched on or near private parts, penetrated against your will by anything, photographed inappropriately or subjected to inappropriate medical treatment. Some "accidental" touch can be purposeful. Also, abuse occurs when sexual activity was consensual, but then one person wants to stop it, and the other refuses.

Sexual Shame: The combination of shame from what happened to the abuser in the past, and feelings of guilt, shame, lust, etc., of the abuser in the present.

Shame: A significant issue in the experience of childhood sexual abuse and/or neglect. It is a powerful feeling of being too defective to be worthy of love. It can show up in the body as a stooped posture and downcast eyes. Healing involves learning to love and accept yourself as you are.

Smokescreen: Something that hides or conceals what is really happening.

Trigger: Something that occurs in the present that sets off a reaction to a past trauma.

Validate: To support and legitimize another person's experience.

Verbal Abuse: Name-calling, threatening, discounting, demanding, accusing, teasing, yelling, and belittling. Embarrassing you in front of others, using obscenities. Statements beginning with, "You always..." and "you never..."